Victorians and Edwardians Abroad

To my mother

Victorians and Edwardians Abroad

The Beginning of the Modern Holiday

Neil Matthews

PEN & SWORD HISTORY

First published in Great Britain in 2016 by
Pen & Sword History
an imprint of
Pen & Sword Books Ltd
47 Church Street
Barnsley
South Yorkshire
S70 2AS

ISBN 978 1 47383 427 9

A CIP catalogue record for this book is available from the British Library

Typeset in Ehrhardt by
Mac Style Ltd, Bridlington, East Yorkshire
Printed and bound in India by Replika Press Pvt. Ltd.

Pen & Sword Books Ltd incorporates the imprints of Pen & Sword
Archaeology, Atlas, Aviation, Battleground, Discovery, Family History,
History, Maritime, Military, Naval, Politics, Railways, Select, Transport, True
Crime, and Fiction, Frontline Books, Leo Cooper, Praetorian Press, Seaforth
Publishing and Wharncliffe.

For a complete list of Pen & Sword titles please contact
PEN & SWORD BOOKS LIMITED
47 Church Street, Barnsley, South Yorkshire, S70 2AS, England
E-mail: enquiries@pen-and-sword.co.uk
Website: www.pen-and-sword.co.uk

Contents

Acknowledgements   vi

Chapter 1   Introduction   1

Chapter 2   The Birth of the Polytechnic   9

Chapter 3   Early Poly Travels and the Origins of the PTA   25

Chapter 4   The Business of Touring   42

Chapter 5   The Outward Journey   53

Chapter 6   Being There: What the Tourists Did   63

Chapter 7   Meeting Jean le Foreigner: What the Tourists Thought   80

Chapter 8   The Purpose of Holidays: A Modern Note?   96

Chapter 9   Conclusion: Independence and War   111

Chapter 10 Afterword   121

A Note About Money   128
Selected Bibliography   129
Index   134

Acknowledgements

Thanks are due to the University of Westminster and to the Quintin Hogg Trust for giving me the opportunity to research the thesis which was the starting point for this book. My principal supervisors Mark Clapson and Tony Gorst provided invaluable advice on many occasions.

All historians owe a debt to archives and their custodians. Within the University, the Archives team of Elaine Penn, Anna McNally, Claire Brunnen and Rebecca Short have been unfailingly helpful. Among the numerous other archivists who have given assistance I am especially grateful to Paul Smith of Thomas Cook; Tony Lees of Manchester County Records Office; Sinead Wheeler of Toynbee Hall; and Paul Wetherall of Manx National Heritage.

Eloise Hansen, Heather Williams and Karyn Burnham at Pen and Sword Books Ltd have been responsive, helpful and supportive editors. Dominic Allen came up with the beautiful cover design.

Finally, the encouragement and support of my long-suffering wife Helen has been, as always, essential.

Chapter 1

Introduction

> All travel has its advantages. If the passenger visits better countries, he may
> learn to improve his own, and if fortune carries him to worse, he may learn
> to enjoy it.
>
> (Samuel Johnson, *Journey to the Western Islands of Scotland*, 1775)

The modern history of holidays for the British people is, perhaps surprisingly,
one of the aspects of travel and tourism on which historians have written
relatively little. Certainly travel in its widest sense has a long, rich and varied
heritage as any reader of Herodotus, Chaucer's *Canterbury Tales* or the tales of
Sir John Mandeville or Marco Polo – or, for that matter, of Samuel Johnson and
James Boswell – will know.

Major motivations for travel have included pilgrimage, commerce, exploration
and colonisation, sometimes in combination and not always initiated by the
British. Witness, for example, two key events of 1735: a French expedition
to attempt to confirm whether the earth was a (Cartesian) perfect sphere or
a (Newtonian) spheroid with flat poles; and the publication of *The System of
Nature* by Carl Linnaeus, a Swedish naturalist, which tried to classify all plants
into one system.

Nonetheless, the British have traditionally played a central role in many
accounts of continental and global travel over the centuries. The obvious
example of this was the network of European journeys known as the Grand
Tour, especially from the late eighteenth century onwards, as the upper classes
sent their sons abroad for a mixture of reasons, which Jeremy Black has
summarised as 'social emulation and a viewpoint of foreign travel as a means
of education and particularly of social finishing'. The wealthiest might go as
far south as Italy, with less affluent travellers staying in France and the Low
Countries, some venturing to Germany and a relatively small number sampling
the delights of Scandinavia and Russia. The view of foreign travel as beneficial

had not always been generally shared: James Boswell's father thought that 'there is nothing to be learned by travelling in France'. After the end of the Napoleonic Wars in 1815, the Grand Tour took on a different flavour, with the educational benefits being a less significant motivator by then. Literary pilgrimages and an appreciation of landscape had become important factors; the latter as part of a wider trend in which the Romanticism of Goethe and Wordsworth's poems and Schiller's plays were prominent. Tourists looked out for the 'picturesque', literally something that would look good in a picture. Later still, they would seek out the 'sublime': the rough, dark, vast, powerful, infinite face of nature which terrified and captivated at the same time.

Travelling through Britain and abroad also came to acquire a reputation for one specific benefit; it could improve your health. The therapeutic advantages of mineral waters have been well known as far back as the Roman era. Over time, medical opinion advocated cold bathing as a care – sometimes regardless of the mineral properties of the waters. Crucially for the development of tourism in Britain, Dr Richard Russell's 1752 book advocated the internal and external use of seawater, in the same way as spa waters. The coast had greater capacity than spas, 'large enough to absorb all comers, and social homogeneity mattered less' as John Pimlott put it. By the mid-nineteenth century, most of Britain's spa resorts – Brighton, Bath, Cheltenham, Hastings, Scarborough, Ramsgate, Margate – were by the seaside. Easy access from main population centres was crucial – Brighton, according to Thackeray, was 'London plus prawns for breakfast and the sea air' – and Blackpool and Southport benefited from direct rail lines. The quality of sea air also assumed significance as a perceived benefit for health. By the mid-nineteenth century, as more of the middle classes holidayed at the English seaside, their social superiors went further afield: to Scotland, Ireland and the Continent. They sought health benefits in Switzerland for example, where cure houses and sanatoria might deal with tuberculosis (also known as consumption). The British started to arrive in greater numbers from around 1875 and played their part in developing Switzerland as a mecca for winter sports. The Tourist Association of Thun stated in 1900: 'Ways must be found to compensate people of quality for having to suffer the presence of the disgusting masses.'

Much of the existing historical research and writing relates to a relatively small and wealthy proportion of the population, but some progress has been made regarding travel and tourism for the majority of the British people. The survival of archive material relating to Thomas Cook, some dating back to the mid-nineteenth century, has enabled various authors to chart the history of that remarkable company and its eponymous founder, all the way back to the historic train journey between Leicester and Loughborough in 1841. Thomas Cook's importance in widening the availability of foreign holidays – especially to that most protean category, the middle classes – has been well acknowledged. Recent research has helped us to learn more about the emergence of holiday camps during the twentieth century, especially under Billy Butlin and Harry Warner before World War II and then after 1945, when they offered affordable and accessible holidays to an over widening range of working people. Eventually, the innovations of coach and air transport and the gradual recovery from the deprivation of wartime coalesced into what is generally called 'mass tourism' (probably in the late 1960s, though a firm consensus on exactly when this fabled era began is elusive).

Even so, the picture is far from complete. Between the Grand Tour and 'mass tourism' – between 1830 and 'Club 18–30', we might say – much is still unknown. Information has not survived in such volume for other travel agencies as it has for Thomas Cook. We may, for example, never know that much about Henry Gaze, whose firm boasted ninety-four offices worldwide by 1890. The campaigner and editor WT Stead wrote about Gaze in the same category as Cook in the 1890s – as substantial and well-established companies. Gaze's sons were, it seems, less capable, or perhaps less fortunate than him in business; the company was bankrupt by 1903. It is, in part, the lack of information on Gaze and other companies that exaggerates the significance of Thomas Cook. Recent researchers have stressed that the original Thomas Cook (1808–1892) did not necessarily invent the railway excursion all by himself, or organise trips to the 1851 Great Exhibition for nearly as many people as has been supposed.

This book is a modest attempt to contribute towards filling the gaps in the overall picture. Its main focus is one of the most enduring and successful travel agencies of the late Victorian and Edwardian era: the Polytechnic Touring Association (PTA) and its parent institution, the Regent Street Polytechnic.

The story of the PTA has lain untold until now in the archives of the University of Westminster – the institution that the Polytechnic eventually became. To trace the Polytechnic's role in the creation of the PTA, we can follow its gestation through the accounts, minutes of the governing body and other committees, membership applications and correspondence. As the PTA grew, it generated brochures, leaflets, guidebooks, memorabilia and other promotional material. Through the pages of the Polytechnic's in-house magazine, we can follow the evolution of the tours both at home and abroad; the Polytechnic's management promoted the tours and Polytechnic tourists reported on them. Private letters and diaries provide further insights into the tourists' views and experiences. For comparative purposes, it is also useful and revealing to look at the records of other travel agencies such as Thomas Cook, the Co-operative Holidays Association, the Holiday Fellowship and the Toynbee Travellers' Club; at the memoirs of key figures from the burgeoning travel and tourism industry; at earlier histories of the Polytechnic and its leaders, and at coverage of the tours in contemporary magazines and newspapers.

The Polytechnic and the PTA were born into a tumultuous time, as the effects of long-term industrialisation and urbanisation changed England forever. For some, this offered new opportunities for 'white collar' working in particular, as well as more leisure time and the temptations of new hobbies and new transport technologies – the personal (bicycles) and the collective (cheap train travel). But this was not a time of unalloyed liberation – far from it. The continuing prevalence of religious observance – whether or not it demonstrated genuine faith – and the seemingly unshakeable power of 'respectability' led Victorians to order and codify their pleasures in many cases, with organised sport a prime example. Holidays themselves came within the ambit of 'rational recreation', as many perceived them to have serious restorative and moral purposes.

By the late Victorian years, Thomas Cook had already shown how a new type of travel agency could bring foreign holidays to at least some of the rising and aspiring middle classes – as well as those already comfortably well-off – with time and money to spare. Where Cook led, others eventually followed; with Henry Lunn's various companies, the Co-operative Holidays Association and the Toynbee Travellers Club most prominent. And, just as the Toynbee Travellers Club emerged from an educational association in the shape of Toynbee Hall, so the PTA was a by-product of the creation and growth of England's first Polytechnic. Inspired by its founder and first President Quintin Hogg, and shaped and led by him and his chief lieutenants Robert Mitchell and JEK Studd, the Polytechnic was a blend of club and classroom for young men (and later young women), whose success persuaded the government to set up other bodies in emulation.

As Hogg's Polytechnic established itself, travel was part of its fabric from its early days. Hogg himself was a regular traveller overseas, with numerous business interests to develop, while other Polytechnic members moved abroad to new lives in the USA, India and elsewhere. Teachers at the Polytechnic led tours to Germany and to France with varying degrees of success. This general interest in travel turned into a more organised Polytechnic programme in the late 1880s. Robert Mitchell was a key figure; in 1888, he created a ground-breaking tour of Switzerland for boys from the Polytechnic's day school and he later arranged the purchase of chalets at Lucerne, which became more closely associated with the Polytechnic and later the PTA than any other destination. While that 1888 trip entered Poly mythology as the origin of the touring operations, the series of Polytechnic groups, which visited the Paris Exposition the following year were, in some respects, just as significant. The idea to visit the event came from the Polytechnic's French Society, emphasising the educational motivation (and the reports of the visits in the Polytechnic's in-house magazine gave an early taste of Poly attitudes to foreigners' and the French in particular).

From these beginnings, a programme of Polytechnic tours began to take shape, with Switzerland and Norway the most popular foreign destinations, followed by Paris – though more adventurous Poly holidaymakers could go to Madeira or even the USA (for the Chicago Expo in 1893). In parallel, with its origins in Hogg and his wife's philanthropic sharing of their holidays with others, the Polytechnic also created a programme of trips within the UK and holiday homes for use by its members, students and poorer members of the local community. The holiday homes and UK tours sprang up first in south-east England, reflecting the Polytechnic's London location, but quickly spread through the British Isles as far as Jersey, Scotland and Ireland.

Crucially, the tours were profitable, providing much-needed funds for an institution that regularly ran annual deficits and relied on external grants and the generosity of Quintin Hogg to survive. While it is not possible to be definitive about the 'typical' Polytechnic tourist, it seems the success of the tours came from tapping the emerging and expanding sectors of office-based and professional workers – although a variety of 'respectable' people including vicars, magistrates and local councillors were willing to offer personal testimonials about their experiences on Poly holidays. The tours attracted customers from around the British Isles and from international organisations such as the Young

Men's Christian Association of North America. They also gained favourable press coverage in praise of the Polytechnic tours' aims and contrasting them with 'regular commercial agencies'. The most famous of these 'regular' agencies, Thomas Cook, complained at government level about the unfair commercial advantage that they felt the Polytechnic tours enjoyed – though, it seems, to little effect.

RL Stevenson famously ventured that 'it is better to travel hopefully than to arrive.' We can discover whether this axiom applied to Polytechnic tourists by examining the accounts they gave of their outward journeys, especially in the Polytechnic's magazine, but also in letters and diaries. In those pre-air travel days, the challenges of crossing the Channel brought some predictable problems, with seasickness being a regular theme. However, if the accounts are to be believed (and the Polytechnic was presumably publishing them for promotional purposes) the outward trip was enjoyable for most. The tourists occupied themselves, and entertained other holidaymakers and locals, with displays of marching and singing, among other activities.

Once they had arrived, the tourists normally found ways to make the most of their holidays. Not surprisingly, the reports of shorter trips, such as day trips to Boulogne, give a frenetic flavour of holidaymakers dashing from sight to sight, keen to make every moment count. The most popular destinations, Switzerland and Norway, offered the chance to escape a workaday urban existence for a short time, as the tourists explored mountains, glaciers and waterfalls among many natural attractions. Whether a few days or a couple of weeks, Polytechnic holidays enabled the tourists to tick off as 'done' the sights they hoped, and were expected to see a form of obtaining, as it were, cultural capital. Stopping on Sunday for a visit to the local church or chapel was a prominent part of many accounts of Poly tours. However, while the tours' origins in educational motives continued to be reflected in what the tour reports mentioned as part of their itineraries, there was plenty of evidence of what one writer called 'a capacity for enjoyment'. Tourists could outwit foreign emperors, annoy German police officers and even get roped into taking part in local cricket matches.

Enjoying their holidays was one thing: but what did Polytechnic tourists think of 'abroad', and the people they encountered there? Their reports of the tours took their cue from the contemporary geopolitical and diplomatic context, with the British Empire close to its zenith and attempting to preserve its position as the principal world power of the time (and the Polytechnic, of course, was based in London, heart of the Empire.) Neither Switzerland nor Norway were serious military or political rivals, but the French certainly were. Perhaps in reaction to this, Polytechnic travel writers took a distinctly superior attitude to their cross-Channel neighbours, portraying Parisians as lazy, uncultured nuisances who would attempt to con them out of their hard-earned money, and French people outside the capital as living in a previous (and hence less threatening) age. Poly tourists enjoyed making an impression on the locals, and travel reports frequently mentioned the ways in which Swiss or Norwegian people greeted them in friendly fashion. Both nationalities gained praise for being honest, industrious, friendly and unlikely to swindle the tourists out of money. Nearer home, travellers to Ireland found the experience a little unsettling, preferring to focus on their own activities such as fishing and hill climbing instead of engaging in discussions with the politically 'sensitive' Irish. Compared with travel accounts in the magazines of other travel organisations such as the Co-operative Holidays Association or the Toynbee Travellers Club, Polytechnic travel accounts conveyed a distinctive 'Poly view' of the rest of the world.

Above all, what was the purpose of travel and holidays? As you might expect, the answer varied depending on who gave it. One significant forum for reflection on this subject was the regular series of 'reunions', which the Polytechnic held for those who had been on specific tours. While the reports of reunions sometimes referred to the educational advantages of the tours, other benefits gained more prominence: the opportunity to refresh oneself, a chance to escape the pressures of modern life, sociability, good fellowship and simple pleasure and enjoyment. While other organisations might stress the possibility for contact with foreign fields to increase international understanding and reduce the risks of future wars, relatively few Polytechnic travel writers seemed to take this view. As the Polytechnic expanded its tours and holiday homes programme, allowing non-members and non-students to join them, the question of how accessible the tours were for members and students became a subject of some contention. The Polytechnic liked to promote itself as pioneering affordable travel, but some members of its community complained that the tours were increasingly unaffordable and inaccessible for the very people they had originally been set up to serve. Occasionally, Hogg and the other Polytechnic leaders even faced accusations that the tours detracted from the institution's main works.

The final two chapters of this book bring the Polytechnic and PTA story up to the brink of war and give a glimpse of what happened afterwards. The PTA became a company limited by shares in 1911, although its links with its parent institution remained close; its owners were Mitchell, Studd and Quintin Hogg's son (Quintin having died in 1903), its offices remained on Polytechnic premises and its articles of association pledged it to help the Polytechnic. Switzerland remained the principal destination for PTA tours along with the UK and continental Europe, for over 16,000 tourists a year.

The advent of the First World War temporarily halted the PTA's progress. After 1918, it had to adapt to a changed world, in which holidaymakers were more likely to travel to southern Europe, to follow the sun, and in coaches and motorcars as they began to supersede trains as the most popular methods of getting there. JEK Studd's son Ronald became Managing Director and steered the company through challenging times, retaining Switzerland at the heart of the portfolio. Promotional materials stressed the importance of personal service, comfort and value for money, with less emphasis on the educational benefits of travel. Ronald Studd remained in charge until well after the Second World War, by which time the popularity of holiday camps in the UK, the development of affordable air travel for foreign holidays, and a slow rise in the amount of paid leave for many working people were combining to bring new opportunities and challenges. In 1962, an aviation entrepreneur acquired Poly Travel (as it was known by then) along with another firm, Sir Henry Lunn Ltd, leading to the eventual creation of a famous travel brand: Lunn Poly.

However, the most innovative and exciting times for the PTA were its early days, as the emerging travel firm helped to send increasing numbers of Victorians and Edwardians abroad. The early history of the Polytechnic, the PTA, and its tourists, forms a tantalising bridge between Victorian ideas of rational recreation – the idea, broadly, that leisure was there to improve you and to 'recreate' you for work – and more modern notions of the purpose of leisure and holidays. While the official channels of the Polytechnic often professed fairly traditional views on how holidays should benefit its customers, the customers themselves sometimes had different ideas. Our conventional ideas of our Victorian and Edwardian forebears are of serious souls but these tourists, in their own way, are closer to us in their enjoyment of holidays than we might imagine.

Chapter 2

The Birth of the Polytechnic

The late Victorian era into which Quintin Hogg's Polytechnic was born contained multitudes and contradictions. Confidence jostled with insecurity; prosperity sat side by side with deprivation; belief co-existed with doubt.

From an economic point of view, industrialisation continued to drive urbanisation and changes in job patterns. While the population of England and Wales rose by sixty per cent between 1851 and 1891, the number of agricultural labourers fell by almost forty per cent, due chiefly to the attractions of urban employment.

While the last quarter of the century witnessed a general economic depression in the agricultural sector, greater prosperity in the rest of the economy offset this decline. Wage earnings may have risen by about ten per cent in the 1880s while retail prices fell by fifteen per cent. This dual pattern continued, albeit more slowly, in the 1890s. Cheaper imports of wheat and meat were a significant factor, along with economies of scale arising from the mass production of some foodstuffs.

Meanwhile, with greater net income there came – for some groups of workers, at least – more voluntary leisure time. While paid holidays for manual workers were still rare, the Bank Holidays Act of 1871 offered some relief from daily toil. Various voluntary agreements in the early 1870s limited working hours in certain sectors to nine per day; in 1874 and 1892, Acts of Parliament limited working weeks for textile workers.

Many of the new jobs that came into being during these years were white-collar occupations such as clerks, commercial travellers, national and local government workers and teachers. The white-collar sector accounted for 130,000 men and 69,000 women in 1851; by 1891 the totals had risen to 500,000 and 194,000 respectively.

White-collar workers comprised one sector of that great mass which sometimes seems to monopolise history – the middle class. The Great Reform Act of 1832 marked one milestone in its growth, with about a third of a million voters added to the electoral roll. By the 1870s and 1880s, the Liberals and Conservatives were selecting more middle-class candidates to stand as MPs. Another sign of these middle-class times was the growth of the professions:

Profession	Numbers in 1861	Numbers in 1901
Clergy	19,200	25,200
Physicians/surgeons	14,500	23,000
Barristers/solicitors	14,400	21,000
Teachers	110,300	230,000
Mining/civil engineers	4,400	11,000
Dentists	1,600	5,300
Accountants	6,300	12,500

As the professions grew, they created professional bodies through which to regulate and defend themselves, such as the Law Society (in 1843) and other institutions for engineers, architects, surveyors, accountants and auditors. As Lawrence James has described, this section of the middle-classes found various ways to gain controls at different levels of public life, whether through overt political representation as described above, professional representation, serving in public roles as magistrates or on juries or setting up, running and supporting voluntary conservation bodies. The Royal Society for the Prevention of Cruelty to Animals, an earlier example (1824), was followed by organisations such as the Society for the Protection of Birds (1889) and the National Trust (1895).

At the same time, on a small scale numerically but influential nonetheless, public schools developed an ideology of sport as a tool with which to keep order, to encourage team spirit and leadership and to train students for imperial service. The rise in the numbers of boys and (from 1870s) girls going to public schools – which were not expensive by the standards of the day – was not a coincidence. Anxious parents wanted to keep their children safe from 'contagion' and teach them the right moral ideals. One businessman with a son at Rugby in 1866 was particularly keen for the boy to learn Classics, not for his own sake but to help him 'keep his position in society'. The reinvention of public schools, which had started with Thomas Arnold becoming headmaster at Rugby in 1828, was part of a wider desire among certain sectors of society to reinforce social barriers, not increase social mobility.

During this period, the English middle-classes 'discovered sport and surprised themselves with their enthusiasms', as one historian puts it. Although, the arcane language and rules of pastimes such as lawn tennis and croquet emphasised exclusivity for those sections of the middle-class who practised them. The new Amateur Athletics Association barred mechanics, artisans and labourers, promoting itself to 'Gentleman Amateurs'.

Breakthroughs in bicycle technology in the 1860s also stimulated great interest, with the foundation of the Cyclists Touring Club in 1878 and the creation of cycling sections of temperance societies and Clarion Clubs. The latter were an outgrowth of the creation by Robert Blatchford (1851–1943) of *The Clarion* newspaper. The Clarion Clubs were active in the growing practice of organised rambling. Cycling itself became a fulcrum for 'rational' debates about the appropriate clothing for women cyclists, and about whether it encouraged healthy, sober habits. Sport became an increasingly visible adjunct to many existing organisations, with teachers, clerks and other white-collar workers as prominent participants in many of the sports clubs, run under the various benevolent eyes of the church, mechanics' institutes or the Young Men's Christian Association (YMCA).

However, the picture was not so rosy for everyone. Victorian society was also increasingly aware of the wide inequalities between 'haves' and 'have-nots'. One manifestation of social reformers' reactions was a wide array of charitable and philanthropic initiatives including Sunday school treats, summer outings, soup kitchens, clothing and coal clubs, Bible classes, temperance societies, boys' brigades and savings banks. Much of this activity came from the churches, no doubt partly as a reaction to increasing evidence of religious scepticism in some quarters. A religious census taken on Sunday 30 March 1851 to ascertain how many people went to church had found that large numbers stayed at home. Nonetheless, denominational statistics for the Victorian era showed a rise in the numbers aligned to the Church of England and to the Methodist, Congregationalist and Baptist sects in England and in the numbers of Roman Catholics in the rest of Britain. Christian revivalism, as preached by DL Moody and others, enjoyed much popularity during these years. The Church of England began to make more frequent use of choirs, to hold more frequent services, to place more emphasis on congregational responses and to provide benches instead of pews. There was a rising level of church involvement in external clubs, societies and associations. Lambeth in the 1890s had thirty-one Anglican and fifty-five major non-Conformist places of worship which supported – among other things – fifty-eight thrift societies, fifty-seven mothers' meetings, thirty-six temperance societies for children and nineteen for adults, thirty-six debating clubs, twenty-seven girls' clubs, twenty-five sports teams and twenty-five penny banks. From day to day, bible readings and morning prayers remained a prominent part of many middle-class lives.

One aspect of the centrality of religion to the lives of many Victorians was a resurgence of interest in Sabbatarianism. Pressure groups including The Society for Promoting the Due Observance of the Lord's Day – commonly called the Lord's Day Observance Society – and the National Lord's Rest Day Association used various tactics to attempt to restrict Sunday activities, with their targets including cheap Sunday railway excursions. In some respects they enjoyed a degree of success, with Sunday opening for the British Museum, the National Gallery and other London museums delayed until 1896. However, Sabbatarianism was, in many ways, a defensive movement.

And, of course, closely allied to religious observance, or outward conformity at least, was the idea of respectability – a key social divider, cutting across classes. House building focused on better plumbing, separate wings of the house for servants and separate bedrooms for children. Middle-class society comprised 'layer upon layer of subclasses', as FML Thompson put it, who knew all too well that a major part of being respectable was to *appear* to be respectable. A section of the working class, as one measure of respectability, subscribed to insurance funds. Religion, as Thompson has explained, it was a central pillar of respectable behaviour, teaching 'piety, chastity, sobriety, filial obedience, and charity, and [it] shunned displays of luxury, sexual transgressions, and all diversions which were not improving or uplifting'.

Respectability linked in turn to one of the preoccupations of the era, namely 'rational recreation' – the idea of regulating the amusement of the lower classes, for their own improvement and to integrate them better into society, and of appeasing middle-class uneasiness about the greater availability of leisure time for themselves. The 'layer upon layer of subclasses' viewed each other with at least a modicum of suspicion, with traditional working-class forms of leisure such as bowling, glee clubs and, of course, public houses coming under scrutiny. Racing, a major working-class interest, was closely associated with gambling, which the authorities feared because they thought debts would lead to theft. Football, traditionally a game of the streets, came under the watchful eye of new police forces.

But, for that section of the middle-class who took up the 'rational recreation' cause, simple surveillance, regulation or prohibition could never be enough. Counter-attractions had to be available, to divert the working-man from his pub and his pigeons. In some cases in the early Victorian era, the counter-attractions came from employers such as Samuel Greg, a Cheshire employer who provided music classes, gardens and tea parties; or Robert Owen's New Lanark mills whose annexe housed a school, a museum, a music hall and a ballroom. The church activity in clubs, associations and societies that we noted earlier was not simply a defensive manoeuvre in order to shore up established religion's position; it was part of the array of counter-attractions.

The 'rational recreation' movement was not totally successful by any means, partly because its intersections with temperance, respectability and religion could create contradictions. How could working-class men be encouraged, for example, to visit art galleries or even the British Museum if they did not open on Sundays, the one non-working day of the week? The Working Men's Club and Institute Union, founded by Henry Solly in 1862, and grown branch by branch in its early years by landlords or clergy, limited its own effectiveness by banning beer from club premises. Tea and coffee were not sufficient refreshment after stints working in the mines. In the end the CIU gave in, beer appeared and the clubs came more under the direct control of working men, who passed their time with programmes of lectures, concerts, games, excursions and picnics. Similarly, attempts to control alcohol consumption in music halls only succeeded to an extent, with drinking restricted to the bar areas. The Coffee Music Hall Company, founded in London 1880 as an arm of the temperance-based coffee public-house movement, found it hard to make ends meet.

Also, as we might expect, acceptance of the 'rational recreation' argument was hardly unanimous within the middle classes either. The Deans' disciplinary books for Oxbridge colleges give plenty of evidence of bad behaviour: gun-shooting in rooms, noisy games, disorderly parties, noisy singing, neglect of chapel and even ignoring the regular curfew. As early as the 1830s there was a middle-class element to the crowds at horse races. As John Pinfold has shown, by the 1880s and 1890s some sporting clubs had started up in Liverpool at private venues, where it would be harder to stop people betting. There were occasional police raids, but perhaps the main priority was to keep betting off the streets. In other words, local society might tolerate 'unrespectable' behaviour if it was out of the public domain. A close-knit local business community could use its discretion to keep some misbehaviour from becoming publicly known. Harriers athletic clubs publicly professed temperance or even abstinence, but some drinking and smoking – for example, at so-called 'smoking concerts' – took place.

Holidays were one aspect of the debate about respectability and 'rational' behaviour. If you could afford them, and had the spare time to go on them, they were not there for carefree enjoyment, or so the conventional wisdom argued. They were a counter-attraction. Holidays could 'improve' the holidaymaker and restore them – 're-create' them – to full health for the main part of their lives: work. In this sense, holidays were one tool in the arsenal of those who advocated 'rational recreation'. However, like the music hall or the pub or the racecourse, a holiday might offer the chance to let one's hair down; to be less than totally 'respectable'. It is not always easy to find records in Victorian newspapers and other archive material of 'unrespectable' behaviour. While Polytechnic holidaymakers might not have disgraced themselves (or at least were not going to put it on record if they had), they did take the opportunity to behave at least a little naughtily, as we shall see later.

The debate about the purpose of holidays and the wider sphere of leisure, and the idea of holidays as being educational and improving, found a focus in the earlier part of the Victorian era in the efforts of perhaps the most famous travel agency ever created: Thomas Cook. The story of the eponymous founder of the firm (1808–1892) has been told many times and needs only a brief summary here. The best-known landmark event of Cook's early efforts in arranging travel took place on 5 July 1841, with a temperance-inspired train journey from Leicester to Loughborough. In later years, Cook's twin beliefs in the benefits of travel and temperance drove him to build his own hotel and a neighbouring temperance hall in Leicester. By the end of the 1850s, he was organising excursions to stately homes such as Belvoir Castle, longer trips to Scotland and Ireland, as well as helping thousands of people to visit the Great Exhibition in 1851. Problems with Scottish railway companies encouraged Cook to look to the Continent by the early 1860s, introducing journeys to Paris and then onwards to Switzerland and Italy – many of the tourists going on personally conducted tours. From there, Cook branched out into American holidays and, by the end of the 1860s, Egypt and the Middle East. He learned the advantages of paying in bulk, allocating rooms in advance and had the germ of the idea for the hotel coupon, a key part of package holidays for years to come. Tourists were happy they couldn't be overcharged, Cook was paid by the tourists before having to pay hotels and the hotels received more custom because more tourists stayed there and ate there. Cook claimed to have organised travel for two million people by the start of 1868 and, by 1892, as many as a thousand people may have gone round the world with the firm. Profits soared to over £20,000 a year.

In Piers Brendon's words, Cook 'regarded tourism as a kind of free trade in people… a form of social enlightenment'. However, the greater availability of holidays, and foreign holidays in particular, attracted criticism from such eminent Victorians as John Ruskin and Henry James – even if the latter did qualify his initial views. Others insisted that 'no man could find in travel anything he did not carry with him', the implication being that an individual needed an education before being able to benefit from extensive travel. As Brendon says, this missed – or chose to ignore – the possibility that travel itself could be educational. In any case, the critics' fears of the social effects of a more widely travelled 'mass' of the population misjudged the profile of Cook's tourists. Many travelled independently, which suggests a degree of prosperity. Cook's clients included clergy, physicians, bankers, civil engineers, merchants, booksellers, chemists, shopkeepers, lawyers, academics, scientists and architects. Their annual incomes were probably in the range of £300–£600. As the firm became established and offered destinations as distant as Australia and New Zealand, it attracted more eminent clients. The firm even organised a trip for the German Kaiser, Wilhelm II, to Jerusalem in 1898. Cook had his advocates within the great and the good: William Gladstone praised the firm for giving thousands of British people the chance to travel 'with great enjoyment, great refreshment, and great improvement to themselves'.

Where Thomas Cook led, with his successful blend of travel, temperance, accessibility and respectability, other travel agencies followed in the latter part of the nineteenth century. John Frame (b.1848 in Lanarkshire, Scotland) drew inspiration from a 'dominie' who had travelled to France, Switzerland and Italy.

Frame's father had wanted him to join the family firm of tailors but, after his father's death, he moved to Preston in Lancashire. Frame, a strong supporter of the temperance movement, initially went into the travel business by organising a two-day travel fare for temperance workers from Preston who were invited to join a choir of 5,000 at the Temperance Festival at Crystal Palace in 1881. From that point, Frame repeated the Crystal Palace tour annually and also ran tours of the Scottish Highlands and of London, as well as day-trips for fans of Preston North End Football Club.

Sir Henry Lunn (1859–1939), the son of Wesleyan Methodists, studied simultaneously for the Methodist ministry and a degree in medicine. Lunn's lifelong interest in church reunion led him to organise a Conference for senior ministers of various churches, in Grindelwald in Switzerland, in 1892. Some of the delegates asked Lunn to organise a tour to Rome; his anticipated party of fifty or sixty for the Easter 1893 trip became 440 in all, generating a healthy profit. Lunn went on to organise cruises to Palestine, Egypt, Athens and Constantinople and to the Greek islands, both including lectures, which became the template for the Hellenic Travellers' Club. Lunn's friendship with a master at Harrow School led him to run holidays to Adelboden in Switzerland for Etonians and Harrovians – the origins of the Public Schools Alpine Sports Club, whose benefits one member summed up as 'the old kind of comradeship which [had] formerly existed in Switzerland' before the country had been 'buried under … mountains of hotels'. During the 1890s, Lunn was also a prominent figure at Quintin Hogg's Polytechnic, as its Chaplain, Speaker of the Polytechnic Parliament and sometime tour leader.

Further north, Thomas Arthur Leonard (1864–1948), minister of a Congregationalist church in Colne, Lancashire, began to organise walking holidays in Lake District for his church's Social Guild Walking Club in the 1890s. His activities derived from his view of the Lancashire wakes – originally religious celebrations or feasts, which had developed into secular holidays whereby local factories, collieries and so on closed for a specific week. Each town in Lancashire took the holiday on a different week during the summer. In Leonard's view, the wakes 'led to thoughtless spending of money, the inane type of amusement and unhealthy over-crowding in lodging houses; moreover, it made for vitiated conceptions of life and conduct and produced permanent effects on character.' Leonard organised a holiday for thirty young men at a house in Ambleside in 1891. Gradually, an unofficial committee of like-minded people coalesced around Leonard and, in 1897, the Co-operative Holidays Association (CHA) was born. A typical CHA holiday lasted a week and featured non-optional rambles during the days, often eighteen to twenty miles long, with lectures, recitals, country dancing and concerts in the evenings. The CHA used empty cottages for accommodation and school halls for communal activity. All holidaymakers undertook basic chores such as boot cleaning and washing up. From 1902 the CHA began to offer trips abroad, initially to Switzerland. CHA membership was mostly middle-class, petit bourgeoisie and higher working-class. This new organisation was linked to the National Home Reading Union (NHRU), whose principal aim was to raise the standard of working-class leisure reading. Along with the increasingly popular cycling and rambling clubs, the CHA's holidays can be seen as part of a reaction against the alienating effects of industrialisation and urbanisation, as well as part of the rational recreation movement.

Last but not least was the closest contemporary parallel to Hogg's Polytechnic, also based in London: Toynbee Hall, named posthumously after Arnold Toynbee (1852–1883), an Oxford historian, but founded by Samuel Barnett (1844–1913), vicar of St Jude's in Whitechapel. The articles of Toynbee Hall committed it to seek 'to provide education and the means of recreation and enjoyment for the people of the poorer districts of London and other great cities'. Within a few short years, the Hall's residents were managing elementary schools and sitting on committees for the promotion of recreational evening classes and on charity organisation society committees, as well as giving lectures to hundreds of students. Barnett believed that the lectures should be 'primarily cultural and not vocational'. Shakespeare, Elizabethan and Antiquarian Societies came into being, as did a volunteer cadet force and a teetotal social club. Toynbee Hall operated a philanthropic holiday fund for the less fortunate. The Children's Country Holiday Fund sent over 17,000 children for a break away from the city in 1888. The Hall had also, by this time, begun to organise annual trips to continental Europe, linked to studies of the destinations, with visits to Belgium in August 1887 and to Florence, Pisa and Genoa in Italy in 1888. After this last expedition, it was decided to form the Toynbee Travellers' Club. Membership was restricted at first to students, residents and associates of Toynbee Hall, but later extended to members of University Extension classes. Months of study of the art and history of the country to be visited preceded each tour, which included lectures. The Club's efforts would, in later years, be augmented and then superseded by the formation of a Workmen's Travelling Club.

Toynbee Hall and Hogg's Polytechnic were inevitably affected by many aspects of the national trends described earlier, which found their reflections in London. Between 240,000 – 440,000 migrants relocated to London in each decade between 1841 and 1891, with many looking for jobs, such as young women seeking positions in domestic service. London's economy did not mirror the national economy exactly, growing more slowly in terms of the manufacturing sector, for example. However, the city was crucial to Britain's increasing world share of international trade, and it was the world's great money market. The numbers of clerks in London trebled in the thirty years to 1891, by which time ten per cent of male Londoners were white-collar workers.

A developing London transport network began to encourage some lower-middle-class and working-class Londoners to move out to the suburbs and commute to work. Steamboats were carrying such 'commuting' traffic by the 1830s; over thirty-seven million passengers travelled with the London General Omnibus Company by 1856–7. The Metropolitan Line, the first on the Underground, opened in 1863 and, by the 1870s, there were around 160 million rail journeys each year within London. Central government had encouraged cheap travel as early as 1844 by specifying that rail companies had to run at least one train a day with a fare of no more than 1d.

Of those Londoners with leisure time, more and more were taking their leisure further and further away from the capital. Margate, Ramsgate and Gravesend had already been popular destinations by steamboat as early as the 1840s, and middle-class Londoners began to discover Brighton by the 1850s. By the 1880s and 1890s Clacton and Southend welcomed visitors from London's East End for a day or for weekends. In his investigations, Charles Booth found growing numbers of clerks, policemen, shop workers and local government workers (who had one to two weeks paid holidays by this time) going to the Sussex, Kent or Essex coasts. Booth and Joseph Rowntree's research suggested that seventy to eighty-five per cent of working class families could afford occasional trips to the seaside. London also acted as a key terminus for increasing numbers of forays to continental Europe, with cross-Channel passages rising from around 165,000 in 1850 to 344,000 in 1869 and 951,000 by 1899.

London was also at the heart of several significant sports developments. Lord's Cricket Ground in Marylebone hosted the meeting of county clubs on 10th December 1889 which made the County Championship official. The following year, the first Championship featured eight teams including Middlesex, Surrey, Sussex and Kent. A group of London clubs created the Football Association in 1863, an important step towards the codification of the game, which opened up further with the participation of northern clubs with mainly working-class memberships in the FA Cup in 1871.

Philanthropy in the capital operated on a massive scale. The 640 London charities active in the 1860s spent between £5.5 million and £7 million each year – more than the annual cost of poor relief in England and Wales. The goal of charity was 'to bring recipients into the fold of society' by encouraging them to adopt middle class virtues – self-help in particular. The Charity Organisation Society was founded in 1869 to coordinate distribution of funds in London.

London was not only the capital of the United Kingdom, but also the centre of the British Empire. However, there was increasing concern about Britain's economic and industrial competitiveness against a rapidly industrialising continental Europe, especially that of Germany, and the USA. The weakness of technical education – which we might nowadays call vocational training – had been the subject of Royal Commissions in 1872–5 and 1882–4. The Polytechnic, and the other institutions created later in its image, were perceived as part of the solution to this problem.

Nobody could better embody the themes of empire, religious devotion, philanthropy and a belief in the social benefits of education and organised sport – not to mention travel – than the Polytechnic's three outstanding figures in its early years. The most important was Quintin Hogg (1845–1903). He was born in London, the fourteenth and youngest child and seventh son of Sir James Hogg, a successful barrister who also served as Chairman of the East India Company. Quintin's older sister Annie regularly read Bible extracts to him and he kept a Bible, given to him by his mother at the young age of ten, throughout his entire life. He went to Eton, where he formed a Bible study group, enjoyed sports and made several friendships, which endured throughout his life. Ironically, the young Quintin did not have a distinguished academic record.

Declining the chance to go to Oxford in favour of a year of travelling, Hogg worked instead for a tea merchant in the City of London. During this time he became interested in the plight of homeless or 'ragged' boys and, with help of friends from his Eton days (Arthur Kinnaird, later Lord Kinnaird (1847–1923) and Thomas HW Pelham (1847–1916)), he started a 'ragged school' near Charing Cross. The endeavour relocated to Castle Street as it grew and Annie began to help him out, holding classes for the sisters and mothers of ragged boys. Hogg became an advocate to emigration as a way to give new opportunities abroad to Englishmen from a disadvantaged background.

By 1870, Hogg's wife Alice (1846–1918) was helping to teach and supervise girls who were housed separately from the boys, while evening classes were available for 'better class' boys. Over the next few years, Hogg established the Youths' Christian Institute and Reading Rooms at 15 Hanover Street, where Hanover United Athletic Club was formed in 1874. In 1878 the Institute moved to Long Acre and was renamed the Young Men's Christian Institute (YMCI). Finally, in 1881, Hogg took an opportunity to buy the Regent Street premises of the Royal Polytechnic Institute, and the YMCI eventually became known as the Polytechnic.

Until his sudden death in 1903, Hogg was the President, benefactor and dominant personality of the Polytechnic. He was a regular international traveller, often on business – personal or Polytechnic-related. Even Quintin and Alice's honeymoon in 1870 was a long trip through America, during which they visited several boys who had emigrated there after an education at Quintin's hands. Hogg had business interests on sugar plantations in Demerara and he was Chairman of the Anglo-Ceylon and General Estates Company, with interests in Ceylon and Mauritius, and other directorships including a post with Sao Paolo Coffee Estates. The YMCI's inhouse magazine *Home Tidings* (later renamed, unromantically, the *Polytechnic Magazine*) published Quintin and Alice's letters about their travels through Italy, India and the Far East at various points during 1879–80. Without Hogg's strong attachment to foreign travel – not to mention his financial support, of which more later – it is hard to see how the Polytechnic would have ventured into providing tours and holiday homes at all. After Hogg's death, his second daughter Ethel Wood (1878–1970) both preserved and enhanced his reputation by writing his biography (as well as that of Mitchell) and a history of the Polytechnic itself.

For much of this period, Robert Mitchell (1855–1933) was one of Hogg's two chief lieutenants. Mitchell was the son of a detective who had worked at the

Great Exhibition in 1851. He grew up in a family who regularly attended chapel and began working life as an apprentice to a metal worker. After going to a bible class held by Hogg, Mitchell became honorary Secretary of what was then called the Institute in 1871, eventually agreeing to become its paid Secretary seven years later and the Polytechnic's Director of Education in 1891. It was Mitchell who drew up the Polytechnic's original scheme of technical education classes. By 1884, demand for technical training was so great that Mitchell arranged 'elementary' trade classes between 7 am and 8 am each day, at a cost of one penny a day, with breakfast included. Mitchell played in the Polytechnic brass band and played the harp and flute. Like Hogg, Mitchell was a keen sportsman, with news of his rowing exploits appearing in *Home Tidings* as early as June 1879. When the Polytechnic became involved in the running of the London Olympics in 1908, Mitchell planned the opening and closing ceremonies and the special display for the visit of the King and Queen and the French President.

Robert Mitchell was a key figure in turning nascent Polytechnic interest in foreign travel into organised tours, and in the purchase of chaléts in Lucerne, and he became a one-third owner of the PTA in 1911. Three of Mitchell's siblings joined the Polytechnic teaching staff; his wife Isabella (1857–1949) managed the Lucerne chaléts for many years, and his son Robert (b.1883) and nephew Basil (b.1888) led Polytechnic/PTA tours.

The life and career of John Edward Kynaston (JEK) Studd (1858–1944), the other key figure in the early Polytechnic years was, in some respects, even more remarkable than those of Hogg or Mitchell. Studd's father, an indigo planter, master of foxhounds and racehorse owner, underwent an evangelical conversion and his three eldest sons followed suit, with JEK's attendance at an American Evangelist meeting in Drury Lane marking a turning point for him. JEK went to Eton and was due to enter a London firm of tea traders, but trained instead as a medical missionary before entering Trinity College Cambridge in 1880. With two of his younger brothers, he gained his 'blue' and played in the Cambridge cricket team that beat the Australians in 1882. He met Quintin Hogg through a religious mission, and Robert Mitchell because they attended the same bible classes. In 1885 he was asked by Hogg to join the work at the Polytechnic. JEK became honorary secretary from 1885, vice-president in 1901 and, from Hogg's death in 1903 until his own in 1944, President of the Polytechnic. He was the third owner, with Douglas Hogg and Mitchell, of the PTA after 1911, as well as being its Chairman and appointing his son Ronald as Managing Director. He was later awarded an OBE, knighted and eventually created a baronet. JEK was at different points Lord Mayor of London, President of the Old Etonian Association and President of the Marylebone Cricket Club (then cricket's ruling body).

The social and moral value of sport and an unshakeable religious belief remained twin obsessions for JEK Studd throughout his life. In one press interview he explained sport as 'a break in the routine and dead level of existence' for many, and contended that 'man is something like a four-cylinder engine. He has a physical engine, a spiritual engine, an intellectual engine and a social engine and it is the business of man to make all four engines run'. Three of his sons and a grandson would later serve as PTA directors.

But all that would be some time in the future. As the 1880s wore on, the task for Hogg, Mitchell and Studd was to establish the nascent 'Polytechnic' – an extraordinary mixture of club, classroom and leisure centre. It served a variety of target markets. Initially, young men from the age of sixteen were eligible to join as members; the upper age limit was twenty-two but, by 1891, this increased to twenty-five or, for ex-members being re-elected, thirty. There was an entrance fee of one shilling, initially as a registration fee to enter the name of a prospective member or candidate in the candidates' register. There were younger boys as well. A Middle-Class School for Boys aged from eight to over-thirteens, with fees per term from £1 to £2, 12s 6d, offered the facilities of chemical and electrical laboratories, engineering and carpentry workshops and the School of Art, in addition to a gymnasium and swimming bath. Meanwhile, the Polytechnic Young Women's Christian Institute (YWCI) was established in 1888, in Langham Place to provide similar educational, social and sporting facilities for women. This built upon the earlier work by Alice Hogg and her sister. Classes had been open to women at Regent Street from the early 1880s in various subjects, some of which (such as art) they could study alongside men. At Langham Place, though, the curriculum included some distinctively 'feminine' subjects such as dressmaking and cookery.

Hogg's Institute had already offered an impressive array of classes at Long Acre, such as mechanical drawing, arithmetic, reading, geometry, grammar, bookkeeping, perspective drawing, French, shorthand, art, geometry, model drawing, freehand drawing, geography, building construction, mental arithmetic and choir practice. At Regent Street, the educational portfolio expanded in several areas. A wider range of options in practical trades, technical and artistic subjects was now on offer. Students could learn musical instruments such as the cornet or the violin. Day classes were held 'for ladies and gentlemen' in English, French, German, Greek, Hindustani, Latin, algebra, natural philosophy, chemistry, geography, writing, grammar, organ, pianoforte, harmony and gymnastics.

The Polytechnic had little trouble attracting both students and members. Even before the move to Regent Street, one issue of *Home Tidings* had listed the names, addresses and occupations of thirty new members, and the names of those members who had proposed them for admittance. Five of the new members were clerks, four were compositors, two were sailors and two were salesmen. Other occupations on the list included: ironworker, bookseller, printer, grocer, collar cutter, woodcarver, upholsterer, gilder, coppersmith, carpenter, instrument maker, book-keeper and cutler. Such diverse lists of new members became a regular feature of *Home Tidings* for the next five years. By 1886, the Polytechnic was styling itself as being 'For Artizans, Apprentices & Others – The Largest Mechanics' Institute in the Kingdom'.

The Polytechnic's social side grew and developed rapidly, too. It was open between 5.30 pm and 10.30 pm every evening except on Sundays and bank holidays. A subscription of 3s per quarter – reduced to 2s per quarter by 1891 – gave members free use of the library and of reading, social, chess and draughts rooms; admission to concerts, entertainments and lectures; the chance to join various clubs and societies; and 'the privilege of joining any of the classes at greatly reduced rates'. In the earliest years, the subscription was 3d per week, with a reduction of 4s per year if the member attended classes on at least twenty-five occasions. A Recreation Ground at Merton Hall was reserved for members' use. In later years, the Polytechnic also created Associate and Honorary Membership categories.

Elected committees of members ran a range of clubs and societies, charging subscriptions and, in some cases, entrance fees. They included trade societies such as Engineering, whose members would sometimes visit large engineering establishments in and around London; sports, such as Hanover United Athletic Club (for which Studd was on the committee, chaired meetings and was captain of cricket) and the Ramblers (of which Studd was President); and military and musical clubs such as the military band, of which Mitchell was President.

This huge range of educational and social activity was regulated tightly and conservatively. Polytechnic rules prohibited smoking, lotteries, gambling, alcohol and 'unbecoming conduct or language', and the discussion of any theological subject without 'the express permission of the Committee,' which also had to approve the formation of any new society along with its rules. 'The Committee' was a small executive management group that made day-to-day, week-to-week management decisions; Hogg and Studd often chaired it, while Mitchell attended regularly.

One constant theme of the early years was financial difficulties. Invariably, income could not cover running costs, including teachers' salaries and teaching apparatus, nor the need for capital investment at Regent Street, as demand for classes continued to grow. The financial deficit reached £9,000 by 1886, with Hogg's personal financial contributions keeping things afloat. Eventually, the Polytechnic was able to source funding from outside its own doors. An 1883 Parliamentary Act had consolidated various London charities under the control of the Charity Commissioners, who could dispense about £60,000 per annum in support of technical and social education. After an energetic eight-year Polytechnic campaign, combining fundraising from its supporters and lobbying of the authorities, the Charity Commissioners agreed to fund the Polytechnic. In 1891 they approved a capital grant of £11,750 and promised an annual grant of £3,500. The annual deficit was by now, as Hogg's daughter Ethel Wood wrote much later, 'well under £2,000, most of which could be raised without great difficulty in the Institute itself, by means of the school, holiday tours, etc'. This last reference to tours was no accident; as we shall see, the burgeoning business of planning holidays for students and members was one of the Polytechnic's few profitable activities.

Chapter 3

Early Poly Travels and the Origins of the PTA

As we have seen, the 1880s was the decade in which the Polytechnic established itself in Regent Street. It found substantial demand for its classes and for its other services, with over 11,000 members and students on the books. Financially, it had survived thanks to Hogg's largesse before achieving formal financial support, and recognition of its status from the Charity Commissioners. The creation of a travel agency was not a part of the plan, insofar as Hogg and his fellow Poly leaders had a plan, but somehow it emerged, within a Polytechnic culture that promoted travel and encouraged members of its community to share their experiences. This chapter looks at how the embryonic PTA came into being, offering holidays both abroad and in the UK.

Even in the earliest years of the Polytechnic, foreign travel was a prominent part of the lives of its members and students. In addition to the teaching of foreign languages, the reading room included travel-related content and speakers included visitors from British colonies. Along with reports from its various sports clubs, bible extracts and new member lists, the organisation featured travel on a regular basis in its inhouse magazine, *Home Tidings*. The December 1879 issue regaled readers with letters Hogg wrote from Italy, en route to India and Ceylon, and announced that a photographic album of images from Italy was available to view. The Hoggs' experiences in India and the Far East took up substantial sections of the magazine in March, June and July of the following year.

Home Tidings was also the medium through which one could learn of members such as Frank Day leaving for a new life in the USA. Members who had already relocated overseas could use the magazine to update their friends on their progress – or lack of it. One of the less optimistic reports came from WH Preece in Calcutta:

At present work here is very bad. I have got a wonderfully good situation, but I only get 80 rupees a month, and this, as you must know, goes a very little way here … so far from this being a city of palaces, I only wish I was out of it; but there are several difficulties in connection with my getting away.

In the same issue, WJ Burridge, stationed with troops in Alexandria, endeavoured to see the bright side: 'It was not all to my liking, but I thought to myself, it's all active service, and I must do something to earn a medal …' Closer to home, *Home Tidings* gave advance notice of a lecture on 'North America and Canada' [sic] and reported on an excursion to Epping Forest in Essex.

In the course of the 1880s, *Home Tidings* published more and more accounts of members' travels within the UK and abroad, which were initially self-organised. An August 1885 report of a journey to Cardiff by steamer stated that the boat's skipper had tried to shoot a penguin 'for his mid-day meal; but … the shot missed its mark'. Whether the penguin was in the river, on its banks, accompanied or escaping from a local zoo was not recorded.

In the same month a German instructor, one Dr Andresen, led a trip to Antwerp's international exhibition, then on to the battlefields of the Franco-Prussian War (in which he had served). Judging from a number of articles and letters in *Home Tidings*, this was less than a total success. The promised fifty per cent discount for the Antwerp exhibition did not materialise; Andresen ran out of Belgian currency in Bruges; problems arose with train times, advertised and actual; and the group missed the steamer home from Ostend, taking instead a vessel to Dover, with the more affluent group members buying everyone's tickets. The resulting financial disputes about who in the group should repay whom – and about 'the miscalculations and extravagance of an incompetent leader' (i.e. Andresen) – rumbled on through *Home Tidings* into May 1886, with a sub-committee formed to investigate. In contrast, an Easter 1886 visit to Paris went well under the aegis of Mr SL Hasluck, an elocution teacher who, a report wryly noted, 'performed the leviathan feat of pleasing every member of the party.' Hasluck repeated the trip the following Easter and also proposed a journey to Switzerland at the end of that July.

Switzerland was the destination for the trip which later became mythologised as the beginning of the PTA. It happened in 1888 as a result of a sudden inspiration by Robert Mitchell. Ethel Wood, in her biography of Mitchell, tells the story thus:

Stopping to listen to a geography lesson [in the day school] *one day, he asked both master and boys if any of them had seen the mountains and glaciers, torrents and waterfalls that were being described. Not one had … In 1888* [Mitchell] *went off to Belgium and Switzerland, planned a walking tour by the simple expedient of following the proposed route on foot himself, cajoled or bewildered railway companies into granting extremely favourable terms, and sent out a party of sixty boys, three masters and a doctor to study the battle-fields of the Franco-German War, and then to make their way to Zermatt while their geography lessons came to life before their eyes. The cost of the twenty-seven days' trip was £5 19s.*

To give an indication of prices relative to today, £5 19s 6d in 1890 was approximately equivalent to £692.52 at 2016 prices. A letter of 29th June sent to boys' parents stated that the itinerary would include Brussels, Waterloo and also 'two days at Metz and Strasbourg - thus making the trip educational as well as enjoyable.' Mitchell was the driving force in planning the tour, and correspondence with parents was approved by the management Committee. The trip departed on 23rd July 1888 and the *Polytechnic Magazine* gave brief updates as the party proceeded on its journey, reporting on 9th August that it was making good progress despite heavy snow.

In the aftermath of the Swiss tour, a lecture by Mitchell was planned for the following January. Deeming the event a success, the Committee decided to send bronze medals to particularly co-operative hotels and 'to Dr Jackson as a token of appreciation for his kindness in filling the post of Honorary Physician [as a volunteer].'

In April 1889, Hogg – who edited the inhouse magazine at this point, its name changed from *Home Tidings* to the *Polytechnic Magazine* – was noting that there had been many enquiries about another Swiss trip, but this time for Polytechnic members. Options were under investigation, with four parties already 'virtually arranged' for July, of 25–30 members each. By late June, preparations were almost complete for sixteen-day tours at a maximum cost of £5 15s, subject to a deposit of £1. The parties would leave on 17, 18 and 19 July, staying at modest hotels due to the expense of accommodation at that time of year – though, *Polytechnic Magazine* assured readers, each person would have a separate bed (by no means a guarantee for every traveller abroad during this period). As in 1888, brief updates followed as the trips proceeded. On 22nd August, the *Magazine* published an account by one of the travellers, describing the stops at Brussels, Strasbourg and Basle before the final destination of Lucerne.

Around the same period that Mitchell's moment of inspiration grew into these trips to Switzerland, the ambitions of one of the Polytechnic's many clubs and societies developed into a major Polytechnic visit to Paris, to coincide with the 1889 Exposition. Polytechnic parties had visited the French capital before: at Easter 1886 under Hasluck, and during Easter of 1887 and 1888. Members of the groups reported on the trips for the *Polytechnic Magazine*. The 1888 trip comprised fourteen members, with the arrangements made by the secretary of a Paris branch of the YMCA. Meanwhile, the Polytechnic's French Society was looking forward to the 1889 Exposition. The Society had formed on 3rd January 1887, and within a year it had grown from its original dozen members to over eighty, with average attendance at the weekly Monday meetings growing from nine to twenty-four. Polytechnic members could join the Society for 6d per quarter; a further charge for entrance to the meetings had been abolished to encourage growth. The principal purpose of the meetings was an educational focus on the French language, with reading, letter-writing and conversation exercises for elementary and advanced groups, though social events also took place.

Like many other Polytechnic clubs and societies, the French Society submitted regular reports of its activities to *Home Tidings* and then the *Polytechnic Magazine*. It was as an addition to one such report on 16 February 1888 that the Society's Honorary Secretary Charles Loxton announced:

PARIS TRIP. Next year we are going to shut up the show for a week, and take a trip to the Paris Exhibition. W. Jones is appointed Treasurer to a fund opened in our Society for the purpose. He will no doubt have something to say for himself next week. I give the rules, which are as follows:

RULES FOR PARIS TRIP.
1. That the Fund be exclusively for members of the French Society.
2. That members are to pay the Subscriptions at the rate of 9d. per week.
3. The Fund to be managed by the Hon. Treasurer, who shall be under the supervision of the Committee of the French Society. The money to be invested in the Polytechnic Bank.

4. This Trip to take place in or about August, 1889, according to the convenience of the majority of members.
5. A General Meeting of Subscribers to be held early in May, 1889, to elect a Committee to make all arrangements.

Any letter left at the Barrier addressed to Mons. W. Jones, will receive immediate attention.

Subsequent reports reminded members of the Society and the wider Polytechnic of this initiative. Within five weeks, Loxton was predicting that 'If a sufficient number join (which is more than probable, judging by the number already paying into the fund) more than one trip may be arranged.'

Exactly how and when the senior Polytechnic leadership concluded that the Exposition visits were too large a project to leave to one of its societies to plan is not clear: but plainly they did. By November, Polytechnic members were reading of the efforts of Mitchell 'who is in Paris making arrangements for our members' excursions to the Exhibition of 1889', in a short report on his negotiations with local authorities to secure beds and other facilities at reasonable prices. Soon afterwards, Hogg announced:

In connection with the Paris trip next year, I may mention that the following classes have booked themselves for the weeks named:- Plumbing Class, second week in July; Building Trades' Classes, second week in August; Carriage Building Classes, first week in July; Rowing Section, last week in August. The instructors of the particular class will, in each case, accompany the party.

The French Society section of that week's *Magazine* did not mention the Paris trip at all – which continued to gain growing attention and interest. Before long, the Polytechnic leadership had to reconsider the scope of the project again. Hogg complained that:

The amount of correspondence in reference to our proposed Paris trip next year is getting somewhat alarming. Letters come in by every post from different parts of the country, from secretaries of clubs, and employers of labour, etc., asking either for advice in arranging similar trips, or else to be permitted to join our own parties. This last request we are quite unable to comply with, owing to the fact that already nearly every week has been secured by one or the other of the sections or the classes. I really advise every member who thinks of going at all to lose no time in entering his name.

Letters in the same issue asked about normal Polytechnic activities during the Exposition and about the costs of staying in Paris for more than one week. Answering the first query, Hogg stated that 'The Institute is practically closed, as far as its ordinary work is concerned, during the Exhibition period.' Answering the second, he listed the 'rules' as: 'First, we provide for those wishing to spend a week. Secondly, we attend to the claims of those asking for another week. Thirdly, non-members, if any room remains, which is not probable.' Not only was the Paris Exposition taking priority over other Polytechnic work, but Hogg was prepared to admit the possibility of selling places to non-members.

The following week, Hogg noted that he had negotiated with the London, Brighton and South Coast Railway for cheap tickets, and that the Polytechnic could now issue tickets to smaller clubs and institutions booking ten or more places. Slowly, gradually, the elements of what would later be a travel agency were beginning to appear. Hogg called on members to help promote the event and offered 'any number of handbills, large bills for posting, placing in windows, etc' to help ensure the Polytechnic did not lose money overall.

The *Polytechnic Magazine*'s extensive coverage of the Paris Exposition between April – July 1889 included advance notes of what members could do and see while in Paris, commentary on various aspects and incidents and comments and letters of thanks from those who went. 'RM' (presumably Mitchell) set the scene in the 25 April issue, by reporting on a preview of the event, which one of the British Commissioners had arranged for him. 'Notes on the Paris Exhibition' struck an ambivalent tone. It looked forward to the 'fabulous' end result which 'will entirely surpass anything of a similar character ever before attempted', while dwelling at length on the chaotic nature of the preparations. The British part of the Liberal Art Section – nearer completion than the rest – was 'well worthy of our country … there is scarcely any handicraft or profession but what has its appointed place'. Mitchell drew special attention to the display of Messrs Cobbett, the cricket-bat makers of Marylebone. However, he also observed that local labourers were obtaining wages at nearly double the standard rate and depicted 'John Bull …

well sucked, as he enters the parlour of the Parisian spider', warning readers that the British section would be closed on Sundays. Mitchell hoped that 'each member will sketch out his [visiting] plans in advance' and promised help to this end through information in the *Magazine* and at social gatherings which would take place for each party, in the week before its departure.

This mixture of anticipation, patriotic pride, anxiety to get value for money, wariness of the exploitative foreigner and eagerness to export Polytechnic values, [as exemplified in craft and sport] ran through the *Polytechnic Magazine* coverage of the Exposition over the next few months. The 9th May issue mentioned a series of fixtures between the Polytechnic's athletes, rowers and cricketers and Parisian teams, which a Mr St Claire (not, it appears, a Polytechnic member but an Englishman based in Paris) had helped to arrange. This expatriate had, according to the *Magazine*, spent much time and effort establishing an athletics club in the city, and had experienced a 'struggle against strong prejudices, national customs, and the natural dislike that the ordinary Parisian entertains for physical exercise' (not that describing Parisians in this way was prejudiced, naturally). The local press and the Minister of Public Instruction had apparently been receptive to Mr St Claire's advocacy of the playing of cricket and other sports in public schools. However, the report noted, the major obstacle to complete success in Mr St Claire's campaign was the absence of a Saturday half-day holiday, as France 'requires for work seven to our five-and-a-half days each week.' The article concluded that 'we one and all wish Mr St Claire "God-speed" in the good work he has taken in hand.'

By the end of the month, 'the Committee of the Polytechnic' was in a position to confirm the locations for accommodation in Paris ('at each centre a representative of the Poly will be in residence, who will meet the parties upon arrival, and generally assist them to make the most of their visit to the French capital') and the details of railway and steamboat journeys to the French capital. The blow-by-blow itinerary for the first day's planned excursion programme, including the Grand Boulevards, the Bastille, the Hotel de Ville and the Louvre, took up three pages.

The first 'batch' of excursionists, ninety boys from the day school, left for Paris on 31st May. As the weekly visits by Polytechnic parties proceeded, the *Magazine* began to reflect on its members' experiences and observations (interspersed, incidentally, with long letters recounting Hogg's travels in the

Far East). Illuminations and firework displays drew praise for their grandness, although there were one or two noteworthy absences from the entertainment:

> *Notwithstanding the prettiness of the sight, it became very tame as time went on, the utter absence of music being very extraordinary. Not a single military band was in the grounds. Evidently the "bosses" of the illuminations had an eye to Protection, and would not permit competition.*

To reinforce the value of following the advice given in previous issues, the 27th June issue reported the overcharging of two members for a lunch, and reminded members of the list of restaurants printed on 30th May, 'both for the quality of the meals served and the prices charged, and we cannot too strongly urge members to be very careful what other houses they use.' The same issue recounted the cautionary tale of two members who paid two francs each, rather than one, for photographs of themselves, due to the 'shrewdness' of the photographer.

In the end, the Polytechnic did not offer places on the 1889 Paris Exposition trips to non-members. Nonetheless, the numbers of Polytechnic visitors – reported as 140 a week by late July 1889, and nearly 2,500 'excursionists' in all – dwarfed the numbers going to Switzerland at the same time. Nor was this a one-off: a special May 1891 *Polytechnic Holiday Guide* reported that 4,000 people had visited Paris the previous year. The Polytechnic's activities in organising official tours abroad were well and truly under way.

As the foreign tours expanded, two countries led the way in terms of popularity: Switzerland and Norway. This was not a case of the Polytechnic 'discovering' them as tourist destinations before anyone else. Albert Smith and the Alpine Club had popularised Switzerland for British visitors; John Ruskin and JMW Turner had drawn attention to its aesthetic qualities (such as the supposed spiritual aspects of its mountains); and English engineers had played a crucial role enhancing the Swiss railway network. Thomas Cook's first Swiss tour had occurred in 1863 and '[t]he least prosperous of Cook's Alpine excursionists had an income in the order of £300 a year', which indicates that, at first, Switzerland was a destination for the wealthy and the comfortably well-off. Some of its attraction was for reasons of health, with cure houses and sanatoria treating tuberculosis, in particular, as we have seen. By the end of the century, winter sports had probably overtaken health as a major motivation for the well-to-do taking holidays in Switzerland. In the case of Norway, British tourism in Norway had strong roots in a longer-term interest in exploring Britons' 'Teutonic heritage' (through the Normans and their Viking origins). As in Switzerland, British engineers played a key role in developing Norwegian railways, and British steamships to Norway were operating by around 1850. By 1887 a tourist in a Bergen hotel noted 559 English or Scottish names in the visitors' book compared with nine Germans, seven Australians, four Danes, three Dutch, two Russians and two Cubans. Contemporary travelogues praised Norwegians as 'a simple people living in harmony with nature and blissfully uncorrupted by the wiles of civilization' and the Norwegian landscape as 'a nostalgic echo of a virginal, unblemished world' almost devoid of people. Norway was also ideal for active sportsmen, especially those who enjoyed shooting and fishing. Between 1850 and 1880, a number of contracts were agreed between local landowners and British sportsmen giving the latter sole sporting rights to an area. Scandinavia was also included in Thomas Cook's tours for the first time.

Overall, the common attraction of Switzerland and Norway was as 'pre-modern', non-urban places in which to escape some of the stresses of modern industrialised life. By the closing years of the century, they had opened up to a wider clientele from further down the social scale – with Polytechnic tours playing a part in this development. The crucial development for the Polytechnic was the purchase of some chalets by Lake Lucerne in 1894. According to the legend as Ethel Wood recounted it, Robert Mitchell was the key instigator, almost by chance:

Mr Mitchell, on a return journey from Rome spent a Sunday at Lucerne. In the course of a walk he stopped at a restaurant for tea, and whilst resting there was struck by the thought of what an ideal place it would be to spend a summer holiday in. He asked the proprietor whether he would consider any terms, and was told that the real owner was in Paris, and desirous of getting rid of the place. He went back to Lucerne, telegraphed an offer, which was accepted also by wire, and on the journey home worked out the expenses, details of arrangements, and advertisements for a week in "Lovely Lucerne" (a popular phrase which originated in the Polytechnic advertisements).

We have no definitive proof of the truth of this story, nor any alternative account of how the Polytechnic bought those chalets. Suffice it to say that Ethel Wood printed the legend and, to coin a phrase, the legend became the facts. In any case, Switzerland quickly became the most popular destination for foreign Polytechnic tours, with Norway a clear but distant second. Out of 5,314 tourists in the 1895 season, 3,202 visited Switzerland and 1,148 went to Norway. The third most popular destination was Paris with 339. Paris featured as a regular target of Polytechnic visits, often for a short break of four or five nights over Easter or Christmas. Louis Graveline, a French teacher, assistant secretary of the Mutual Improvement Society and secretary of the French Society, led tours to northern France, including five parties in the Augusts of 1901, 1902 and 1903, and one to Belgium. Herr Seifert, a German master, led at least seven annual tours to Germany that also took place in August – presumably because he, like Graveline, would be free of teaching commitments at that time. However, not every regular Polytechnic tour derived from top-down planning or explicit links to teaching staff expertise. Mr WE Spry-East took groups to Boulogne for a summer weekend for at least eleven successive years up to 1900. The first Polytechnic tour to Normandy, in 1894, was a 'special educational' tour under the aegis of the Reading Circle. Organised excursions to the Belgian Ardennes were inspired by a 'pioneer' visit by members of the Ramblers Club in June 1891. The *Polytechnic Magazine* noted that the subsequent centrally organised trip to that region was partly an attempt to meet excess demand for tours to Norway, and that many members were unable to obtain more than one week's holiday at a time.

While north-western continental Europe was where most Polytechnic tourists chose to go for their foreign holidays, there was a wider choice available. An apparent desire among some members to essay a sea voyage had gained the credit for motivating the maiden Polytechnic voyage to Madeira in 1890 for a fortnight for £9 9s, or three weeks for £11, with members' friends, male or female, paying an additional 7s 6d. The Polytechnic authorities claimed that 'The usual fare to Maderia [sic] and back alone is twenty guineas … For teachers and others who can afford this amount, the holiday will be of an exceptional character.' Provision for spaces for the two parties on this trip increased from an initial ten per party to twenty-one; by the following year, the *Polytechnic Magazine* was announcing the likelihood of three parties a month through June, July and probably August. By

1897, tourists with a seafaring bent could take Polytechnic cruises to the capitals and major cities of northern Europe, including St Petersburg, Christiania (Oslo), Copenhagen, Stockholm and Hamburg. The other regular continental destination in the late 1890s was Rome, initially announced in 1894 as a 'cheap educational tour' and generally visited at Easter or Christmas. The Easter break was also convenient for trips that the institution ran specifically for its students, such as in 1899 when architecture students visited Rouen in France and German students toured the Rhine area.

The Polytechnic promoted itself as providing 'affordable' travel – but it offered relatively expensive foreign holidays as well, either directly or through others. The 1895 tours brochure – the earliest surviving brochure from the Polytechnic – emphasised that its tours were not for those 'who can well afford to avail themselves of the more expensive arrangements of well-known tourist agents'. But this did not stop the same brochure advertising a month's cruise of the western Mediterranean for thirty guineas, and a month's cruise of the eastern Mediterranean including the Holy Land, Egypt, Constantinople and Athens for between thirty and sixty guineas (depending on whether the client wished to share their cabin or not). It also offered four variations on a ten guinea holiday to Switzerland for members of that year's Grindelwald conference for which, as in the previous three years, Henry Lunn was the organiser. The western Mediterranean cruise was advertised as being led by Mr Woolrych Perowne, whose name cropped up two years later as the leader of Lunn's Christmas cruise to Palestine and Egypt. That 1897 brochure also gave a preliminary taste of 'one or more Personally Conducted Parties' on summer holiday tours of the United States and Canada, with the arrangements in the hands of Mr L Newton Smith, who was based at the 'Bureau of Travel, International Committee of the Young Men's Christian Associations' in New York. Members would be able to 'extend their Tour to any length desired.' The brochure editorial explained that the complete range of tours was 'calculated to suit a varied clientele'. A handwritten note in the Polytechnic's Reading Circle Scrapbook refers to two thirty-three-day Holy Land cruises due to run in January and February 1899, at a cost of forty-one guineas per head (though the cruises did not, the note added, take place).

We will return to the promotion of tours in more detail later, but one of the most striking aspects of the 1895 and 1897 brochures is their tone of confidence.

The front cover of each listed the members of the Polytechnic's Governing Body – including the Rt Hon AJ Mundella MP and the Rt Hon Lord Reay, to name but two – lending an immediate air of authority. Even as early as 1895 the Polytechnic was trumpeting the 'unparalleled success' of its Swiss tours, which it attributed to satisfied customers both returning for another Poly holiday and spreading the word to others. To back up these claims, it published testimonials by various passengers from cruises that took place during 1894. A passenger from the cruise departing on 1 July praised the excursion as offering 'a store of health for the body, instruction for the mind, and refreshment for the spirit'; the 28 July cruise was 'a marvel of cheapness and management'. Another passenger reflected: 'Long live the Polytechnic and its officials to organise and carry on such useful work at such reasonable rates!' Two years later, the editorial proclaimed that 'The phenomenal success of the Polytechnic Tours, in which over 20,000 persons have taken part over the past four years, renders any detailed preface unnecessary.' (Naturally this was the introduction to a detailed preface.)

It is not only the editorial content, but also the advertising, which helps to give us a picture of the type of people who might go on Poly holidays. They might buy jams, jellies or marmalade from ET Pink of Staple Street, or go to William Kingsmill of Store Street, off Bedford Square, for 'best quality of meat… families and shipping orders will have prompt personal attention… quality guaranteed and prices low'. If joining one of the cruises, passengers could reinforce their temperance credentials with Fry's pure concentrated cocoa. Alternatively, tourists might find, as one advertisement for a brand still going strong today put it, that:

> Holidays make great demands on their physical energy… a recuperative beverage is absolutely necessary. BOVRIL, the vital principle of Prime Ox Beef, provides meat and drink at one draught… [it] is prepared by a special process, which retains the entire nourishing as well as the stimulating properties of the Beef, thereby differing from ordinary Meat Extracts…

Deep pockets would be also be essential, in more than one sense, if tourists shopped with James Lancaster & Son of Birmingham. According to their advertisement, 'Every Traveller should carry a Field Glass or Telescope; an Aneroid Barometer for mountain climbing, and a Pedometer for walking excursions.' Mariners' compasses were available for between 2s 6d and 7s 6d; depending on their power and quality, field glasses could cost as little as 15s or as much as £4 4s.

Perhaps no trip symbolised the scale of the Polytechnic's ambition for its touring operations so well as the journey across the Atlantic, to the World's Fair in Chicago in 1893. In contrast to the serendipitous growth of the 1889 Paris Exposition trip, this was the result of careful Polytechnic preparation over a long period. Members and students knew about the possibility in 1891 and interest was strong even at an early stage. A lengthy update on the planning, published in the *Polytechnic Magazine* on 30 October, stated that:

> *THOSE of our members who have made up their minds to take part in the proposed excursion to the World's Fair in 1893 will be glad to know that the committee have just concluded a contract with the Inman Line for the conveyance of the different parties by the*
>
> *"City of Paris"*
> *"City of New York"*
> *"City of Chicago"*
> *"City of Berlin"*
>
> *The steamers of this line have accomplished the journey under six days; our parties will, therefore, be able to have a fortnight on American and Canadian soil, probably visiting New York, Philadelphia, Washington, Chicago, Niagara Falls, together with a journey down the Hudson River, and home again within a month – an immense boon to those to whom time is an object.*

The Polytechnic hoped to keep the cost of the trip down to twenty-five guineas per head. In notable contrast to Mitchell's disparaging previews of the organisation of the Paris event of 1889, this time *Magazine* readers learned that 'The preparations are being carried out on a scale never before known, and with such mavellous [sic] precision that the very day appointed for the starting of the work of erecting the buildings, found the ground ready.' Reflecting the Polytechnic's own recent creation of a Young Women's Institute, the article revealed that the Chicago event would include 'A noble building, designed by a woman architect… devoted to a complete exposition of woman's work and capabilities.' The event was likely to include significant participation by Mexico, central and South America. In addition, 'China and Japan, whose recent activities have been so obviously a result of the advancement and influence of the United States, will quite outdo themselves.' However, as a sign that the trip would have its lighter side, the article also mentioned plans to include:

> [A] huge swing, 360 feet high, driven by an electric motor, and having a car big enough to contain twenty-four people. The car will travel a distance of 900 feet in ten seconds, or at the rate of a mile a minute, and at its lowest point it will be but two or three feet from the ground, while at its highest it will be 340 feet. Before the delirious attractions of this swing the delights of the switchback railway and the toboggan slide are confidently expected to pale their ineffectual fires. As a producer of dizziness and sickness – sensations of which many people nowadays seem to be strangely enamoured – it should be superior to anything that has yet been devised!

Not all in the Polytechnic community were necessarily enthusiastic about the Chicago trip. On the following page of that issue, 'Scribner' criticised the general public – 'Americans in particular' – for being in such a rush that modern transportation had to take risks in order to meet the greater expectations of speedy travel: 'Lightning express trains across continents and racers upon the oceans are necessities of the day.'

Nonetheless, Mitchell and Quintin Hogg's son Douglas travelled to America in early 1892 to meet officials from the Exposition and to advance preparations for the following year. Among other things, as Mitchell and Douglas Hogg pointed out, early negotiations would help to keep ticket prices down, beating the rush of demand from other quarters. In an extended letter from Chicago, Mitchell told his readers that the compartments in the train which took them from New York to Chicago via the Hudson Valley were 'not only of the most comfortable character, but were heated throughout by steam, and were provided with every comfort imaginable for the journey… [helping to create] an almost perfect service.'

Perhaps the comfort and enjoyment of this reconnaissance trip was some compensation for the stress Mitchell experienced in 1893 when he and his wife went out to the USA in advance of the first party. On arrival in New York, Mitchell found that the railroads had refused to grant the concessions on which the ticket prices for the whole endeavour depended. If the trips went ahead without these concessions, large losses would result which Hogg would have to cover. Ethel Wood's *History of the Polytechnic* takes up the story:

Without a sign of anxiety or distress, Mitchell met the [first tour] *party on arrival and proceeded to show them New York with his usual infectious good humour and enthusiasm. In due course he purchased tickets at full rates for the party to Philadelphia, not, however, at the station, but at a city agency. From Philadelphia he transported them in similar fashion to Washington, still outwardly calm and cheery. The railway companies of course knew the advertised cost of the Poly trip, and seeing Mitchell's unconcerned and steady progress, came to the conclusion that someone must be disregarding the compact.*

The night before he was due to move on to Chicago he was approached by one of the companies and asked how he was obtaining cheap rail tickets. Mitchell smilingly refused any information except that nearly 2,000 people would be travelling on his arrangements during the season. Before the railway representative left him Mitchell had magnanimously agreed to take 500 tickets then and there from his particular organisation at the rates on which the trip had been calculated, and thereafter the other companies were only too glad to accept business on the same terms.

Thus, (according to the legend, anyway) did Mitchell avoid catastrophe. No doubt Hogg would have picked up the tab but, if Mitchell's 'magnificent piece of bluff', as Wood calls it, had failed, the tours' burgeoning reputation might have suffered serious damage.

Meanwhile, plans for trips within the United Kingdom, and the use of holiday homes both for members and for some poor members of the Polytechnic's local community, were maturing. These had their origins back in the early 1870s – precisely in August 1872, when a small house at 24 Portland Place, East Cliff, Brighton was taken for some of the boys in the care of Quintin and Alice Hogg. From then on 'the boys shared whatever autumn holiday plans Mr and Mrs Hogg made'. Even at this early stage, philanthropy was part of the motivation for organising Polytechnic holidays.

By 1887, the Polytechnic's senior leadership was considering options for UK-based short breaks for members, albeit by publicising what was available rather than actively organising it. The following May, Mitchell agreed to find out the cost of hiring a houseboat on the Norfolk Broads, while a house would be rented during July and August for the young women of the Polytechnic. Discussions took place at subsequent management committee meetings about negotiations with the owner of Beacon House in Selsey-on-Sea, Sussex and about the offer of a house in Folkestone (with Hogg deciding to pay a personal visit to the property in each case).

By early 1890, plans were afoot – with Mitchell visiting properties and negotiating with their owners – to rent a summer holiday home in Hastings and accommodation at Clacton 'or some other similar seaside resort'. Given the Polytechnic's London location, it was predictable enough that the earliest UK holiday homes should be in the south-east of England. In fact the first properties on the south coast were at Brighton and Hastings in Sussex, & Ramsgate in Kent and, to the east, Clacton-on-Sea in Essex. The Brighton home catered initially for unmarried members, but soon offered its facilities to working-men and their families at 13s per week for adults and 6s for under-fifteens. The Polytechnic continued to send the children of poor families to Brighton, with 112 children enjoying a seaside trip in 1893. By 1901 the *Polytechnic Magazine* was advertising two Brighton holiday homes: one for young men and the other, a 'temperance boarding establishment', for members generally. Hastings had initially been a holiday home for members of the Sisters' Institute, who could pay 1s a week into a Holiday Fund towards a fee of 20s for one week's stay or 35s for a fortnight. The fee was reduced later and non-members could stay for a week for 16s 6d. In 1895, however, a lack of bookings led the Polytechnic to offer places at the Hastings holiday home to young men as well as to young ladies.

Like Hastings, the Ramsgate holiday home had been early in opening its doors to young ladies. By 1893, the Polytechnic had secured two buildings, one for ladies and one for young men to replace the use of Ascham College at Clacton-on-Sea. Three years later, a few married couples were also welcomed to Ramsgate. The Polytechnic's use of holiday homes in Brighton, Hastings and Ramsgate followed a clear pattern; an initial plan to use each home for a specific, segregated section of the Polytechnic community, which widened in pragmatic fashion later.

From this basis, the network of holiday homes grew. Linton House in Eastbourne, Sussex was in use from 1893 and, eight years later, an ex-Polytechnic member advertised his Hastings holiday home. Gradually, more homes opened for business outside the south-east. So great was the demand for places at the Jersey home and the concern that 'all the places should be snapped up by outsiders [i.e. non-members]', that Hogg took direct action to reserve places for members; and an Isle of Man home was also set up. A new holiday home at Weston-super-Mare, in Somerset, opened in 1894 'at the desire of the Institute Council', and a special Council sub-committee was set up to manage a home in Scarborough.

Along with the network of holiday homes grew a programme of tours and cruises within the British Isles. Killarney in Ireland – with Dublin as a stop along the way – was a regular part of early Polytechnic tour programmes. Initially, specific weeks were reserved for the Sisters' Institute and other weeks for other members or students. Ireland, like Switzerland and Norway, was well-established by this stage as a popular destination for English tourists. Ten new books or guidebooks about Ireland had been published each year in the wake of the Famine, along with hundreds of travel accounts. Killarney, already a well-known location before the Famine, saw a significant increase in the number of tour parties visiting it afterwards. In addition, a number of Polytechnic tours – for members, for architecture and engineering students or for a mixture of members and students – crossed the border into Scotland. In contrast, very few forays into Wales appear to have been attempted; perhaps because few, if any, members booked places when they were organised. Those with a yearning for yachting could do so on the Solent for as little as £2 10s a week, while deeper pockets and more leisure time could secure a fourteen-day cruise around Britain for nine and a half guineas.

The UK holiday homes also became a focus for Polytechnic philanthropy. In 1889 the combined efforts of members, the boys and girls of the Day Schools and 'members of the evening congregation' had raised money for a fund that had enabled about 400 poor children from the Marylebone area to have a week or fortnight away from home in the country or at the seaside. The following year, an article in the *Polytechnic Magazine* suggested repeating this initiative, with swimmers, gymnasts and rowers putting on special events to help raise money for the fund. The Holiday by Proxy Fund would remain a feature of Polytechnic life for years to come, providing holidays for hundreds of the less fortunate every year – as many as 600 people in 1902 at a total cost of £500.

Chapter 4

The Business of Touring

Encouragingly for the Polytechnic, its early official tours at home and abroad appeared to have a sound financial footing. Details of income and expenditure for the year to 30th June 1891 included touring income and costs for the first time. A handwritten note opposite the details of the trip to Killarney in Ireland stated: 'This is the only trip on wh. we lost money – this year we shall make some.'

The tours continued to grow into the new century. Although the evidence is patchy – tourist numbers and financial records survive for some years, but not for others – Switzerland clearly remained the most popular place for a Poly holiday, accounting for more than half of all tour numbers in 1901 (5,290 out of 8,758) and 1904 (6,482 out of 11,394). The numbers going on cruises fell slightly, from 1,531 to 1,134, in the same period. Scotland attracted a consistent figure – around the 1,300 mark each year; Paris accounted for over 1,000 a year by 1904; and the balance consisted of 'sundries' and a visit to the St Louis Exhibition in 1904. In terms of other UK destinations, these seem to have varied in terms of popularity from year to year if we look at the accounts, with Folkestone, Scarborough, Jersey and Penzance featuring at different times.

The touring operations not only generated numbers; they were profitable, too. Swiss tours often accounted for over half of all 'continental and general' income, and sometimes for more than two-thirds. They also generated a great deal of the profits with tours of Paris and the Rhine being the most substantial contributors in terms of income after Switzerland. Of the other components of 'continental and general tours', which generated much less income, holidays in Scotland, Ireland and the Isle of Man saw consistent but small surpluses; tours of Sweden generally broke even. The UK holiday homes created less than £1,000 per annum in terms of income and either broke even or made a small loss. In contrast, the cruises – originally described in the 1902 accounts as 'Norway, Baltic and British Isles cruises', in later years as 'Norway and Baltic', 'Norway and British' and, by

Four key players in the PTA's early years. Quintin Hogg (top left), whose vision, leadership and financial support created and sustained the Polytechnic; Robert Mitchell (top right), who organised and often led the tours; JEK Studd (bottom left), who with Hogg and Mitchell led the Polytechnic; and Scott Durrant (bottom right), who personally led many of the tours

The early Polytechnic years: a typing class (top left); a Council meeting (top right); a science class (above); and female fencers (right).

POLYTECHNIC MAGAZINE

WEEKLY JOURNAL OF
YOUNG MEN'S CHRISTIAN INSTITUTE
309 REGENT ST. W.
PIONEER INSTITUTE FOR

THE POLYTECHNIC
YOUNG WOMEN'S CHRISTIAN INSTITUTE
15 LANGHAM PLACE. W.
TECHNICAL EDUCATION

| VOL. XIII.—No. 265. | AUGUST 9, 1888. | PRICE ONE PENNY. |

President QUINTIN HOGG, Esq.

C. THOMAS. delt.

CONTENTS.

	PAGE
COMING EVENTS	1, 81
INSTITUTE GOSSIP	81—86
THE GREAT KINGSBURY PUZZLE	87, 88
THE ISTHMIAN CITY	89, 91
THE POLYTECHNIC UNION	91
OUR SISTERS' INSTITUTE	91
SOCIETY AND CLUB REPORTS	92, 93
EXCHANGE AND MART COLUMN	93
BANK HOLIDAY SPORTS	93, 95
POLYTECHNIC HARRIERS	95
A MERRY EVENING WITH A MESMERIST	95
POLYTECHNIC Y.M.C. INSTITUTE	96

COMING EVENTS

THURSDAY, August 9th.—Shorthand Society, in Club-room, at 8.——German Society, in Room 10, at 8.30.——Volunteer Drill, in Great Hall, at 8.——Boxing Club, important Committee Meeting, at 9.

SATURDAY, 11th.—Second Party leave for Pluckley, Kent.——Cricket and Lawn Tennis, at Merton Hall, Wimbledon.——Boating at Barnes.——Ramblers to Chislehurst.——Cycling Club Run. (See notice-board.)

SUNDAY, 12th.—Bible Class (Mr. Mark Guy Pearce), in Great Hall, at 3.15, with Orchestral and Organ Accompaniment to Hymns (Young Men only).——Evangelistic Service, General Anderson, R.A., at 7.

MONDAY, 13th.—French Society, in Club-room, at 8.30.——Grand Swimming Entertainment, in Swimming Bath, at 8.

TUESDAY, 14th.—Mesmeric Entertainment by Professor Redman, in Great Hall, at 8.15. Prices as usual.——Mutual Improvement Society, in Club-room, at 8.

OUR SISTERS' INSTITUTE.

THURSDAY, 9th.—Missionary Working Party's Meeting, in Parlour, at 8.30.

FRIDAY, 10th.—Swimming Practice in Bath. Entrance 11, Cavendish Place.

SUNDAY, 12th.—Mrs. Studd's Bible Class, at 3.15, in Room 1.

TUESDAY, 14th.—Professor Redman's Mesmeric Entertainment in the Great Hall, at 8.—Mutual Improvement Society's Meeting, in Room 1, at 8.30.

INSTITUTE GOSSIP

Communications for THE POLYTECHNIC MAGAZINE *must be left in the Editor's Box at the Polytechnic, as early as convenient, but certainly before 10 o'clock on* SATURDAY *Evening, or they will be too late for the week's issue. Only very short paragraphs or notices can be inserted if sent in after the above hour.*

ON Tuesday last, as announced, H.R.H. the Princess Frederica presented the successful candidates of our St. John Ambulance Classes with the Certificates and Medallions they had won.

ON Monday, in spite of the heavy rain which had rendered cricket on Saturday an impossibility, a numerous company attended at Merton Hall, Wimbledon, to see the contest for the prizes offered by the Pedestrian Section of the Polytechnic Athletic Club. A full account of the meeting will be found in another column.

THE postponed general meeting of the Polytechnic French Society will be held in the Club-room, on Monday, August 13th, at 8.30 p.m. As important business will be discussed, all members are requested to attend.

I AM again indebted to Geoffrey Thomas for the new heading which appears for the first time this issue. It is entirely his own design and execution, and I am glad to know that it is thought so good by those capable of judging, that had he needed work he could have obtained plenty of it on the strength of the ability evinced in this job.

I CONTINUE to hear good news of our Swiss Party, who, after being snowed up for a day at Andermalt, the snow falling fourteen hours incessantly, started at eleven o'clock on Friday for the Farea Pass, Rhone Glacier Hotel, a distance of over twenty-seven miles. The snow was fully three feet deep in most places. I am glad to say, that although guides and all the people at Andermalt said the journey was impossible, the Poly. boys "scored a record" and executed "the impossible," reaching their destination about nine p.m., where they were very kindly received and made thoroughly comfortable. The last news were that they were starting for Oberwauld.

IN Mr. Woodhall's letter, dated August 2nd, he gives an account of the party's walk from Andermalt to the Rhone Glacier Hotel, and mentions passing over the Devil's Bridge. Our boys, therefore, have the satisfaction of being one of the last parties to have passed over that wonderful structure. The bridge fell in on Tuesday, August 7th. We shall all be very thankful that the bridge fell in on the 7th, instead of the 2nd.

Swiss pioneers: the 9 August 1888 issue of the *Polytechnic Magazine* reported on the 'Poly boys' journey to Switzerland which the PTA later mythologized as its first tour.

POLYTECHNIC MAGAZINE

WEEKLY JOURNAL OF
.: YOUNG MEN'S :.
CHRISTIAN INSTITUTE
.: 309 REGENT ST. W. :.
PIONEER INSTITUTE FOR

THE POLYTECHNIC
.: YOUNG WOMEN'S :.
CHRISTIAN INSTITUTE,
15 LANGHAM PLACE. W.
TECHNICAL EDUCATION

| Vol. XVI.— No. 363. | JUNE 26, 1890. | PRICE TWOPENCE. |

President, QUINTIN HOGG, Esq.

[Registered at the G.P.O. as a Newspaper.]

Poly. Members at Play.

———o———

HOLIDAY TOURS AND HOLIDAY HOMES, 1890.

"ALL work and no play makes Jack a dull boy"—so runs one of the homely saws of our grandmothers' days; and I fancy few of us, in anticipation of coming holidays, will care to enquire too closely how much truth modern scepticism and iconoclasm concede to the old adage. It is quite sufficient that we feel the need of *some* change from the ordinary run of daily life and work ; so we will not quarrel about words, but "splitting the difference," call it "change of occupation."

FIRST let me enumerate the various sections :—

PAGE

1. HOLIDAY BY PROXY FUND 418
2. CLACTON-ON-SEA HOLIDAY BRANCH 405
3. HASTINGS HOLIDAY HOME FOR MEMBERS OF THE SISTERS' INSTITUTE 406
4. EDINBORO' (including the EXHIBITION AND FORTH BRIDGE), the TROSSACHS, GLASGOW, etc. ... 406
5. SWITZERLAND 408
6. MADEIRA 413
7. SPECIAL SEASIDE ARRANGEMENTS FOR MARRIED MEMBERS 416
8. DEAL SEASIDE CAMP 416
9. BRIGHTON. 417
10. DUBLIN AND THE LAKES OF KILLARNEY ... 419

I will deal with each separately, mainly in the order given.

THE Institute committee have ever been mindful of holiday necessities ; and, for several years have been casting about for ways and means to secure suitable openings for members and students. In 1888 a start was made —it is now a matter of ancient history —with excursions to Switzerland, and last year these were specially organised, extended, and supplemented by weekly jaunts to the Paris exhibition. The experiment has been successful beyond all anticipation. That our fellows appreciated the opportunities thus afforded them of rubbing off some of the angles of their British insularity, was evidenced by the fact of over 2,500 sharing in the ventures last season. For a beginning this was very satisfactory. But "nothing succeeds like success," and it is hardly a matter for surprise that the outcome of last year's operations has this year encouraged the committee to go much farther and wider afield, so that the facilities for holiday-making, change, and rest, now being offered to members, are, as a matter of fact, increased more than fourfold. In every case the aim has been to make the arrangements self-supporting. Not a penny has been asked in charitable contribution, and members may enter fully into our arrangements without feeling under the slightest obligation to anyone. The specially low rates offered are due, simply and solely, to co-operation and Institute organization, of which the committee are glad to give members full advantage as well in matters of play as in those of education and work.

CLACTON-ON-SEA HOLIDAY HOME.

Hon. Surgeon, ANDREW CLARK, Esq., F.R.C.P.

ASCHAM COLLEGE, situate in the best part of Clacton, and commanding fine sea views, has been secured by the committee for August, and a part of September. Very good accommodation for 30 members each week is provided. By the kindness of Mr. E. J. Gilders, land-agent, Clacton, a fine cricket and lawn tennis ground, immediately adjoining the house, will be placed at the exclusive use of visitors. Interesting and enjoyable excursions, at very cheap rates, may be made both by sea and land to various places of note in the district. Mr. J. Deas will be in charge of the arrangements, and everything will be done to ensure a very pleasant holiday for any of our members who may avail themselves of the facilities offered.

Ascham College, Clacton-on-Sea.

MEMBERS going to Clacton will be able to travel either by rail or water, and tickets will be issued at cheap rates. The first party will start on Saturday, August 2nd, and afterwards on each Saturday in August. Terms for the week, including board and lodging, 18s. A few members' friends may be booked upon payment of an extra 3s. per week. Places may now be secured for each week, upon deposit of 5s.

SINCE writing these notes I hear that applications are coming in fast for this and, indeed, for all the excursions enumerated in the present issue. There should, therefore, be not the slightest delay on the part of intending applicants.

Growing at home and abroad: as this special issue of the Polytechnic Magazine from 26 June 1890 shows, holiday options for Poly members and students now included Clacton in England, Edinburgh in Scotland, Switzerland and Madeira.

The 1905 PTA brochure proudly claimed that the Poly and the PTA were 'the PIONEERS of the Co-operative Holiday movement', with more than 13,000 customers every year

The Quadrangle, Polytechnic Châlet, etc.

Wehrli A.-G., Kilchberg-Zürich.

Arrived here safely on Saturday evening about 9 o'clk. It was a very long journey, & rather tiring, for the train ride is monotonous through France, nothing nice to see, but one is amply repaid here. Hope all are well.

Postkarte.

The Revd Rev. Bg.
Upholder,
Conway Road
Colwyn Bay
N. Wales

LUZERN
1.IX.07—9
BRF. AUFG.

Polytechnic Châlet, Gardens and Pilatus

Luzern – Polytechnic Châlet, Gardens on Lake front.

le superbe rebend, Jan 2 Bab
dinners affernoon the scenery
is enchanting, helps 1905
M. Harmer

Lucerne — Polytechnic Chalets and Pilatus

Hasis a lovely large park a little

Adresse

Master Wm Jordes
The Castle
Felton RSO
England

ACC 2808/21

Posted on top of
Mount Rigi in
delightful weather.

This is a delightful
place & we are so
thoroughly enjoying
ourselves Be good
till we get back &
take care of your
arms. Kiss Baby &
Ev for me Your own
Daddy J.D.

Lucerne — Polytechnic Chalets

2/6/06

Arrived safely.
It is just struck 10 o'clock
as (Su-Su) by the boat for left & reach

We're in the lovely
to the scenery to
boat at Lucerne

Steamboat Pier. Polytechnic Chalets.

We have just arrived 9 pt
had a splendid journey all the
way.   Chas E. M.

Seeburg. Polytechnic Chalets.

The Avenue. Lake Front Polytechnic Chalets.

19/6/0x   Lucerne Switzerland
Just come up a cliff railway
& have a beautiful view in front

Luzern, Seeburg mit Pilatus

Lucerne. Polytechnic Chalets, Promenade Lake front.

Lucerne. Polytechnic Chalets. The Old Doorway.

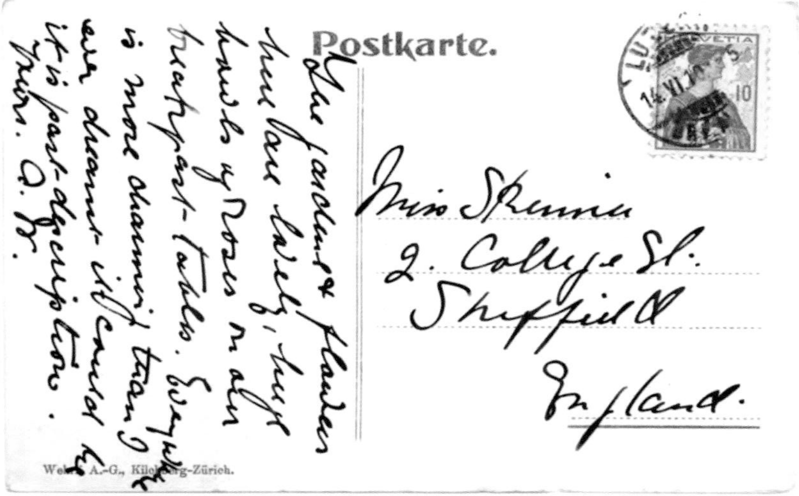
Postkarte.
The gardens & flowers here are lovely, huge bowls of roses on our breakfast-tables. Everywhere is more charming than I ever dreamt it could be, it is past-description.
Mrs. A. B.
Miss Skinner
2. College St:
Sheffield
England.
Webe A.-G., Kilchberg-Zürich.

E. KLEIN, STATIONER, STADTHOF, LUCERNE - DÉP.
Polytechnic Chalets, Seeburg. (Lucerne)
The Chalet Seeburg Lucerne
We are having a grand time & enjoying it thoroughly. Just off to the Rigi. Tomorrow we go up Pilatus. I am sure this place would just suit you. We have splendid weather but it has been very cold here until now. I think you would like to hear how we were progressing. Love from

Zürich vom Polytechnikum aus.

June 5th 1912.

THE OLD FOUNTAIN, THE CHALETS SEEBURG, LUCERNE.

102/5

11642 Lucerne — Polytechnic Chalets

Luzern. Schweizerhofquai mit Pilatus

Globetrotter A.-G., Kunstv...

Mrs Gardiner
9 Panmure St.
Montrose,
North Scotland

LUZERN 2
20. VIII 1936

Dear Mr Gardiner

..... will be surprised to
here I have landed here! We arrived
Sunday morning after a long
journey. Thought I would like to
compare the scenery with our own
My Hubby and Jas encouraged
me. We sailed on the
Lake to-day, and go again
to-morrow Thursday. to Fluelin
at the head of Lake. It is all very
beautiful. We go on to Paris on
Sat. for day. Regards to all J. Simpson

Polytechnic Chalet Seeburg

Dear Father,
Sunday night.
We arrived safely
this morning. It was
raining all the way up
to here. We had to
travel 10 hrs in the
train with the carriage
window open - all along
the Rhine valley. Weather
bright & sunny. We are
in the chalet now & all
the chalet is very comfortable.
Going to Rome for a trip
tomorrow. We are going
there & we shall have
a lovely time. Am breaking
off now.

Love from us here.
England.

580 Verlag O. Wyrsch, Wabern b. B...

LUZERN 2
9-II
12. VII
1937
BRIEFVERSAND

Schweizerische
Unteroffizierstage
LUZERN
16.-19. J...

Mr A. Baldwin.
4 Spring Bank,
Barnardford,
Nr Nelson.
England.

1508 Polytechnic Chalets Seeburg Lucerne

Polytechnic Chalets, Lucerne — Chalet Beau Site

SEEBURG

Boat and Bathing Houses.   Polytechnic Chalets.

Seeburg.   Polytechnic Chalets.

Lucerne-Seeburg. — London-Polytechnic. Schönegg with terrasse.

Polytechnic Chalets Seeburg
Lucern

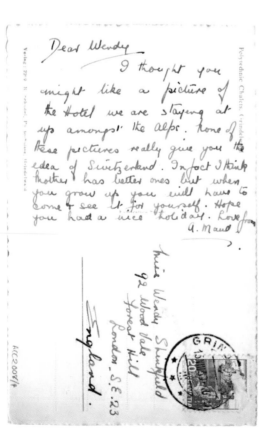

Dear Wendy

　　　　I thought you
might like a picture of
the Hotel we are staying at
up amongst the Alps. None of
these pictures really give you the
idea of Switzerland. In fact I think
Mother has better ones but when
you grow up you will have to
come & see it for yourself. Hope
you had a nice holiday. Love from
　　　　　　　　　a. Maud

Miss Wendy Shurfield
42 Wood Vale
Forest Hill
London. S.E.23
England.

Polytechnic Chalets, Grindel
Verlag: 2779 R. Schnell, Photo-Atelier, Grindelwald
KCC 2.009/f

Interlaken. Polytechnic Chalet

THE DEVILS BRIDGE.

1905, as simply 'Norway' – raised far less income and eventually became a drain on finances. The annual balances deteriorated from consistent small surpluses – never more than £2,000 – to substantial losses between 1908 and 1911. The majority of costs related to the *SY Ceylon*, with around £6,000 each year being allocated equally between wages and repairs, and later to the *SY Viking*, which had been bought to replace the *Ceylon*. By 1910, the Polytechnic's accountants were advising that 'the Tours [could be] placed on a paying basis' if cruising losses were eliminated.

Overall, for 1895–6 and 1901–06 there was a consistently healthy surplus on PTA operations. Part of the surplus became a 'donation' to Polytechnic funds, which in most years amounted to £3,000. The rest of the annual surplus was allocated in various manners, with the most frequent destination for funds being Lucerne, to help to pay off the mortgage on the chaléts (on which £5,662 was spent in 1902) or for some other unspecified reasons, perhaps including substantial repairs or capital investment (£3,520 in 1904, £1,174 in 1905 and £6,070 in 1906). However, things did not go so well between 1907 and 1911, with a much smaller surplus in the first years, followed by four consecutive deficits. The cause of the change of fortune from surpluses to deficits was plain: the deficits came from cruise operations. The one exception was arguably 1910, when a 'Hotel Purchase' sub-account recorded the spending of £3,243 to buy a hotel in Fort William, Scotland, and a further £1,012 to buy a hotel in Killarney, Ireland.

The need for the tours to be profitable becomes more obvious when we look at the accounts for the Polytechnic as a whole. In the seven years leading up to the Charity Commissioners' £11,750 one–off capital grant in 1891 (and its promise of annual grants thereafter), the Polytechnic lost £76,467 – almost £11,000 a year on average. Throughout the later 1890s and well into the first decade of the new century, regular annual deficits continued, with the educational department being the largest loss-making section. Regular grants from the city parochial charities helped to offset this, as did donations from Hogg (for example, £4,000 in 1897 and £3,000 a year from 1898–1902) and others such as Studd. But Polytechnic finances remained in deficit year in, year out, throughout the 1900s. The PTA was the only part of Polytechnic operations that made a regular profit.

So, who were the Polytechnic tourists and where did they come from? This question is hard to answer. No systematic records of the names of tourists survive. There is occasional evidence of the Polytechnic running tours for large groups from outside its own community, such as 250 'mostly students and teachers' from Manchester who visited the Paris Exhibition in 1900. One or two references in travel accounts are suggestive. Travelling to Lucerne a few months after the death of Quintin Hogg, his widow Alice noted:

> *Our second week was made specially interesting by the arrival of a large party of Yorkshire miners and colliers under the leadership of Mr Hibbert. They had been inspired some years ago, by hearing this gentleman give some lantern lectures, with an earnest desire to visit Switzerland, and after saving part of their wages for four years, they had at last been able to carry out this wish.*

The assigning of 'special interest' to the presence of manual workers, and the effort needed to save up for over four years for a cheap overseas holiday, indicates that Polytechnic tours did not attract many from the lowest ends of the socio-economic spectrum. On the other hand, two years later and also in Lucerne, Wilfred Bryant wrote home to his father:

> *At meals I have on my right a Lancashire lad but he has a friend with him – but on my left is an elderly lady & her husband with whom I can talk interestingly at every meal. They hail from Dunstable. Opposite me are a lady & Gentleman from Natal – next to them an uncultivated Swansea man & his wife. You would be surprised at the endless variety of station – age – education, wealth & experience.*

At various stages, Bryant's letters also referred to a curate, a City worker and an architect, all members of the tour party. However, the observations of Alice Hogg and Bryant are anecdotal. In order to gain a more substantive impression of the types of people who went on Polytechnic tours, we have two types of source: membership and candidate records, and lists of holidaymakers.

In the case of membership records, the *Polytechnic Magazine* carried updates from time to time on the overall profile of its membership and the Polytechnic's management was sometimes obliged to divulge such information to external funding or regulatory bodies. In addition, the entries in the registers of candidates for the YMCI and YWCI gave the candidates' occupations. Of course, candidature did not guarantee membership nor, if the candidate became a member, did it guarantee long membership; and there is no direct link between membership and going on Polytechnic holidays. Also, it is not clear whether the occupational categories are self-described. Nonetheless, as the Polytechnic's members were its most obvious and captive target market for the tours, the candidate information is useful, particularly in ascertaining whether there may have been a change in the overall membership profile over a period of years.

A random sample of one page of candidates per month from the registers of candidates for the YMCI and for the YWCI over the period 1891–1911 (or 1905–11 for the latter) yields some revealing patterns. The data sample for men covers 5,079 candidates, with over 170 different occupations; the data sample for women covers 1,055 candidates, with over 50 different occupations.

For the male candidates, one occupational category dominates: that of clerk, which accounts for 2,137 candidates, or approximately forty-two per cent of the total. The addition of similar office-based occupations such as bookkeeper, cashier, civil servant, private secretary and accountant brings this up to forty-five per cent. The next largest category group may be broadly labelled 'those in training' (student, apprentice, assistant) and accounts for just over eleven per cent. Other significant category groups included fashion (e.g. tailor, draper) with eight per cent; construction (e.g. bricklayer, builder, carpenter, decorator, electrician, joiner, plumber) also with eight per cent; retail and sales (e.g. butcher, chemist, grocer) with four per cent; unskilled manual workers (e.g. porter, warehouseman) with three per cent; domestic service (e.g. butler, footman, valet, cook) with two per cent; and printing (e.g. compositor, printer) with two per cent. Occupations that we might classify as the 'lower professions', including architect, draughtsman, engineer, photographer, surveyor and teacher, only made up six per cent of the total. Salesmen (one and a half per cent) are the best-represented within the myriad sub-categories accounting for the remaining eleven per cent.

The data sample, and the variety of occupations, is smaller for the female candidates. Nevertheless, similar patterns emerge. The largest individual occupational category is, as with the men, that of clerk, accounting for twenty-two per cent. Adding other office-based jobs such as bookkeeper, cashier, civil servant, secretary, stenographer, telegraphist, telephonist, shorthand typist and general typist brings this category group to forty-one per cent. The other significant category groups for female candidates include fashion (e.g. draper, dressmaker, embroideress, milliner, tailor) with twenty-seven per cent; retail and sales (e.g. florist, hairdresser, saleswoman, shop assistant, showroom staff, waitress) with eight per cent; 'those in training' (apprentice, assistant, student) with six per cent; and domestic service (e.g. cook, governess, housekeeper, housemaid, ladies' maid) also with six per cent. In a slight contrast with the figures for male candidates, the 'lower professions' (e.g. journalist, nurse, photographer, teacher) make up just under nine per cent, with miscellaneous sub-categories in the remaining three per cent.

The occupational profile of candidates revealed in this data sampling seems to fit broadly with other statistical information about the Polytechnic's member and student numbers during this period. An article in the *Polytechnic Magazine* in mid-1890 reported that, of 8,700 'members … enrolled as members or candidates', 'Clerks and others' accounted for 2,054 of the total, with the next largest category Building Trades (1,754). In 1905, the clerk of governors told the Charity Commission that 'the various classes of men who join the Institute [comprised] Clerks and kindred positions thirty-five per cent, Mechanics 20%, Warehousemen, Drapers & Shop Assistants, Travellers, Porters, etc 40% [and] Others 5%'. Therefore, it would appear that the Polytechnic community – candidates, members and students – broadly comprised the two main elements of the emerging lower middle classes: 'the classic petty bourgeoisie of shopkeepers and small businessmen [and] the new white collar salaried occupations', as Geoffrey Crossick puts it.

However, it is not easy to form firm conclusions about incomes, whether gross or disposable. Even if we focus solely on clerks, the dominant theme of their working experience in this period was diversity. By 1909, when £160 per annum was the threshold above which income tax was payable, forty-six per cent of clerks in insurance, forty-four per cent of those in banking and thirty-seven per cent of those in central government earned more than this figure – but only twenty-eight per cent of those in local government, twenty-three per cent of those in industry and commerce and a mere ten per cent of railway clerks did so. Some clerks had specialised work and were well educated, from better social backgrounds, with good promotion prospects; others, often youths or 'junior' clerks, did routine work. The introduction of pay scales meant that length of tenure was a key determinant of income. In the Civil Service in the years up to 1914, one category of clerks could earn between £70 and £300 per annum while another category earned between £55 and £150. Elsewhere, a 'first-class' clerk might earn up to £400 per annum.

There are two surviving examples of the second source type, holidaymaker lists. The Polytechnic's 1897 brochure included the names and addresses of ninety 'Honorary Referees [who] would be willing to reply to any communications from persons in their district who might desire independent testimony of the arrangements'. The referees included eight councillors, three JPs and two Reverends. The list was overwhelmingly male, with only one Mrs and seven Misses included. Geographically, the best-represented region was the North-West of England with twenty-four referees including seven from Manchester, the best-represented town or city. Fourteen referees were based in the North-East and ten in the Midlands, with the balance spread between the South-East, the South-West, East Anglia, Scotland, Wales and Ireland. Only two referees came from London. The occupations of eight referees can be found in the 1891 and 1901 censuses: Ernest Cummins, a 19-year-old commercial clerk from Bristol; Henry Wilch, an insurance clerk, aged 20, from Norwich; John Callenso, a 22-year-old compositor from Penzance; J Dukes, a 40-year-old watchmaker and jeweller from Aylesbury; T Warburton, a 48-year-old cotton bleacher (described in brackets as 'manager') from Bolton; Alex Grace, a flour and grain merchant aged 63 from Bristol; Alex Gill, a 48-year-old builder from Didsbury; and T Butter, a clerk at a dye works, aged 50, from Perth.

Six years later, appended to a report in a *Polytechnic Magazine* holiday supplement of a cruise to Norway, departing from Grimsby, were the names and home-towns of 166 individuals who had joined the trip. Ninety-four of the party were male (including six Reverends); of these, forty-nine were listed singly. Of the seventy-two women, forty-three were titled Miss and 29 Mrs; thirty-six Misses and ten Mrs were listed as being unaccompanied by men. In geographical terms, seventy-five came from central London or its immediate suburbs, with a further sixteen from the South-East (including three from the Isle of Wight). The bulk of the rest came from the North-West (twenty-four), the North-East (fourteen), the Midlands (ten), Scotland (eight) and the South-West (six). It is impossible to know the proportion of the passengers who were Polytechnic members or students, although the report's author claimed that most had travelled with the Polytechnic before, on the same boat (the *Ceylon*) to Norway or Russia. However, we may safely assume that at least a reasonable proportion were members or students, given the inclusion of the passenger list at the end of the report (and, perhaps, the high proportion of passengers from London).

The 1897 and 1903 referee/passenger lists only represent a small fraction of the thousands who travelled with the Polytechnic in the 1890s and 1900s. Nonetheless, there are points of interest: the 'respectable' element as represented by the Reverends, the councillors and the JPs; the lower-middle class occupational profile of the few referees with traceable addresses; the predominantly male aspect of both groups, particularly the referees; and the high proportion of passengers on the Norway cruise who travelled from London and the South-East to the departure point in Grimsby.

The other point is, of course, the national spread of the passengers' and referees' addresses. This indicates that the Polytechnic had considerable success in widening the appeal of its tours beyond its own community of students and members. This may have been a result of the efforts of Polytechnic staff, members and others to promote the tours. W Scott Durrant, a clerk and tax assessor (later Deputy Accountant-General) who was also active in the French Society, Rambling Club, German Society and Mutual Improvement Society, led tours to Norway, Normandy, the Mediterranean and the Tyrolese Alps. He also lectured about them outside the Polytechnic, to organisations such as the Calthorpe Mutual Improvement Society, the Lancaster Road Wesleyan Church Guild, the Woolwich Polytechnic and, further afield geographically, the Wakefield Mechanics Institute. Frank Beer, a Polytechnic mathematics teacher 'who has personally conducted many of the Polytechnic tours to Italy', addressed the Henley Science & Art School prizegiving, exhibition and public meeting on the sights of the major Italian cities. Frank Short, described in the *Bristol Mercury* as 'provincial secretary, London Polytechnic tours', entertained an audience with a speech on 'An Ideal Cruise in Norway', during which 'Beautiful limelight views were thrown on the sheet, and the lecturer was frequently applauded.'

Short was one of the earliest of a network of local agents, based around the UK, who sold tickets on behalf of the Polytechnic and, frequently, other travel agencies, too. Mr W Madge of Southsea used the local press to publicise the summer 1892 and 1893 programme of Polytechnic tours and to state that he 'would be pleased to be of any service to intending passengers.' Henry Kilner of New Street, Huddersfield, claimed in a local newspaper advertisement that he could supply 'EXCURSION AND TOURIST TICKETS' to various UK locations and tickets for parties conducted to the Continent both by the Polytechnic and by Dean & Dawson. H Samson Clark (1868–1925), who for many years edited the *Polytechnic Magazine*, also acted as advertising agent for the institution, placing advertisements for both its educational facilities and its holiday tours. In August 1896, the first of 24–26 weekly runs of one-inch advertisements for the Swiss tours appeared in the *Scotsman*, the *Yorkshire Post*, the *Western Morning News* and the *Western Mail*.

Even in the early years, the Polytechnic's tours attracted attention at a national level. By 1892, the Polytechnic and Toynbee Hall's travel initiatives had caught the attention of WT Stead (1849–1912), a pioneering investigative journalist. Stead's publicising of an 1883 London Congregational Union pamphlet *The Bitter Cry of Outcast London*, which drew attention to the levels of urban poverty and its attendant misery, had been one of the inspirations for the founding of Toynbee Hall. Stead analysed the Polytechnic and the Toynbee Travellers' Club's travel operations in an article for the magazine he edited, *Review of Reviews*. He cast them both in sharp relief against 'regular commercial agencies' such as Thomas Cook and Henry Gaze who, in Stead's view, served the day-trippers and the 'vulgar' English tourists who merely went abroad to demonstrate their own superiority. In contrast, the Polytechnic and the Toynbee Travellers' Club had opened up the world to:

> *many among the working classes (in the broader sense of the term), men and women of hard-working lives, moderate purses, simple tastes, modest assumptions, and willingness to learn … a deeper and wider comprehension of historical and human solidarity, and with a quickened, humbler, and more passionate perception of the quiet unobtrusive beauty lying hidden away both in external Nature and in human nature in many a highway and byway of their native land.*

The Toynbee Travellers Club, in particular, had used 'co-operative principles' in widening the scope of the original plan for the 1888 trip to Italy – which was to have been limited to Genoa – into a wider cultural and historical tour, which students on other Toynbee Hall courses besides the Italian group could join. Stead covered the Polytechnic tours in less depth than the Toynbee Travellers' Club and argued that the subsequent 'bond of union' between those who travelled together could not be as strong in Polytechnic groups, because of the far greater numbers involved. However, Stead concluded that the Polytechnic and the Toynbee Travellers Club had been founded by Etonians, making Eton:

> [the] *indirect parent of a far-reaching and thoroughly democratic educational movement, furnishing the means on the one hand of academic education in art and European history to working men and women, comparatively limited in numbers, who needed but to be furnished with the opportunity to claim it gladly; and, on the other, of recreational education to several thousands of the workers in the artisan and so-called lower middle class dwelling in those great towns which are commonly regarded as hide-bound in Philistinism.*

In a postscript to the article, Stead profiled the Grindelwald Conference being planned for the first time that year by Henry Lunn, describing it as:

> [A] *definite outgrowth of the Co-operative Holiday movement. Dr Lunn had himself conducted one of the Polytechnic Norway parties, and it was during this voyage that the idea first occurred to him of persuading a number of ministers to join in a common holiday.*

Lunn himself, incidentally, had described that Norway trip in an article for the *Review of Reviews* in 1891. Stead noted that the Grindelwald arrangements would cost Lunn over £1,000 personally, thereby placing the Grindelwald Conference's non-commercial driving force alongside the similarly non-profit-based motivations of the Polytechnic tours and the Toynbee Travellers Club.

Other national and local media offered glowing praise for the Polytechnic and for its burgeoning holiday business. Fred McKenzie, writing in the *Windsor Magazine* in October 1898, noted that 'The Polytechnic differs from most of its English imitators in being distinctively a religious institution' – but that its students and members were free to ignore this aspect of the institution if they wished. It was 'the pioneer of the co-operative holiday movement', with national and international connections:

> *A number of young peoples' [sic] institutes throughout the country have affiliated themselves to the tourist section of the Polytechnic, and the International*

Committee of the Young Men's Christian Association of North America arranges all its European tours through the Regent Street body.

The following year, the *Sheffield and Rotherham Independent* offered an explanation of the need for holidays for all, placing the Polytechnic in the vanguard of providers:

The great tourist agencies, Polytechnic tours, the Co-operative Holidays Association, and many more holiday associations, are making real holidays possible to the people, and vast numbers avail themselves of these opportunities each year ... The annual week or fortnight of tramping or stimulating idleness gives a zest to the working lives of most of us, and sends a refreshing influence through every day of the coming year... everyone agrees that it must be a real change, that we must be lifted out of the well-worn ruts of daily life and be made to realise that there are other corners of the world than ours... We must have more holidays, and ever more holidays if the populations of industrial England are to keep up physique and health. The leisured rich class will always have the pick of the globe to roam over; but every Englishman can nowadays at least get a thorough knowledge of his own country, if proper use is made of the advantages which are increasing every day.

The Isle of Man seems to have been a strong focus for much of the Polytechnic's promotional activities – and the tours made a favourable impression. The *Isle of Man Examiner* (5 August 1899) reported that Mr and Mrs Spence from Douglas, along with Mrs Spence's sister, had gone to Lucerne with the Polytechnic and 'the arrangements made on behalf of their parties... could not be improved upon'. The article revealed that the Polytechnic was planning a Lucerne trip for 'Manx people', departing on 15th September of that year. Four years later, the *Manx Sun* summarised the discussions of the annual meeting of the Belvedere Temperance Hotel Company Ltd, which was struggling to make ends meet. One of the shareholders, a Mr Corlett, argued that 'something should be done to bring the advantages of the hotel before such institutions as the London Polytechnic and Cook's, with a view to getting some share of their business.' JT Cowell, a director of the company, replied that negotiations were taking place with the Polytechnic, which he hoped 'would benefit [the hotel] considerably'.

The Polytechnic was certainly keen to promote and differentiate itself and emphasise its educational (and hence 'rational') motives. The introduction to its 1895 brochure stated the tours were:

> [A]*rranged upon Co-operative principles and, except for those taking part in them, are of no financial benefit to any individual. They are organised with a view to the educational advantages they afford, as well as on account of the delightful holiday they offer. The committee were the pioneers of the now popular "Co-operative and Educational Holiday Movement" And were the first to offer facilities for Continental Travel at such reduced rates as to enable many of limited means to take a holiday abroad. These arrangements are now being largely imitated even by the Tourist Agencies who exerted strenuous efforts to prevent these concessions being obtained.*

Who were these 'Tourist Agencies' apparently trying to hobble the Poly and its tours? This may well be a reference to Thomas Cook. John Cook, the firm's Managing Director, seems to have been determined to obtain government action in order to eliminate what he saw as the Polytechnic's unfair advantage. A letter of 5th August 1897 from Hogg to the Department of Science and Art sought to reply to two letters from Cook to Sir John Gorst, Vice-President of the Government's Committee on Education. In his riposte, Hogg denied that Government money was used to subsidise the tours and stated that the tours were 'financed by me… All wages for additional time [on tour work] are paid by me, and special clerks are engaged at my expense during the busy season'. Hogg bore any loss, but profits were handed to the Polytechnic, whose members received special concessions. The Tours could 'scarcely be described as a department of the Polytechnic at all'. As we have seen, the Polytechnic was by now receiving Government funding, which would otherwise have had to come from Hogg – making it easier for him to finance the tours. There was probably more than an element of truth to Cook's claims, whatever Hogg might protest to the contrary. However, there is no evidence that the Government took any action on the complaints.

So, during the mid-1890s the Polytechnic's tours aimed at, and attracted, a national audience and profile. The next chapter will look at what happened on the tours themselves – starting with the outward journey.

Chapter 5

The Outward Journey

So far, we have explored some of the economic and social trends of late Victorian England, and particularly London, which were coming together to create more opportunities for leisure, including holidays, for more people – and, at the same time, to create Quintin Hogg's Polytechnic in Regent Street. Chapter 3 described the gradual growth of Polytechnic holidays and the ways in which the institution promoted them and profiled the Polytechnic community and the types of people who would go on its tours.

The fact that the Polytechnic *was* a community in itself is the major reason why we have a good idea of what the tourists themselves did on their holidays, and what they thought of it all. Students and members could keep up with news of the tours, as well as other Polytechnic matters, in the inhouse magazine *Home Tidings*, later called the *Polytechnic Magazine*: published weekly for much of this period, then monthly in the early twentieth century. The magazine published a regular flow of letters and articles from tour organisers and participants. These sources, along with a small number of private letters and diaries, are invaluable for our understanding of the tours. However, before we begin to examine them, we should acknowledge they have certain limitations.

Firstly, the contents of the Polytechnic's own magazine were, by definition, selective. While the regular features and, as we shall see later, the letters column provided scope for debate and disagreement, any magazine of this type is bound to reflect the values and beliefs of those who run the institution. Whether 'unsuitable' content was omitted (and Quintin Hogg himself edited the magazine for at least some part of its early years), or contributors and potential contributors exercised, in effect, self-censorship in editing their words before submitting them for publication, the reader received a partial picture, not the whole truth. This point also applies, predictably, to the occasional testimonial, which appeared in promotional brochures.

Secondly, the tour accounts in *Home Tidings*, and later the *Polytechnic Magazine*, often had two particular characteristics: semi-anonymous authorship and a largely male perspective. Many of the authors were tutors who led the tours, such as Robert Avey Ward, director of the school of chemistry. In other cases, the authors used pseudonyms such as BALLYHOOLEY, ONE WHO WENT or THE PASSENGER WHO ENJOYED THE TRIP MOST, or simply initials. These anonymising devices lent a collective, institutional tone to their writings. Although it is impossible to be definitive, it seems likely that virtually all Polytechnic reports of foreign travel were the work of men. There were exceptions: one unnamed author wrote about a 'Young Women's Branch' stay at Ramsgate; and a lengthy female-authored letter about climbing Carrantuohill, the highest mountain in Ireland, was included in the Sisters' Institute sub-section of the magazine. Women were certainly part of Polytechnic tours, but almost never reported them. Alice Hogg's letters from personal travels to the Middle East were published in the Sisters' Institute sub-section. Given the Polytechnic's origins as a young men's institute, and the absence of female contributors from most sections of the magazine, the male bias of the travel accounts is not surprising. (In contrast, female travel authors were a regular presence in the pages of the CHA's inhouse magazine *Comradeship*, while a twenty-fifth anniversary publication for the Toynbee Travellers' Club showed that over fifty per cent of its members in that period were female, and women compiled, or helped to compile, most of the tour logbooks then in the Club's possession.)

Nonetheless, despite these caveats, the travel accounts are a fascinating, entertaining and revealing source as in helping us to imagine holidays just over 100 years ago. So let's begin at the beginning: the outward journey.

Naturally the route varied, depending on the destination, and getting there took a day or more. Going south to Paris for Easter 1887, 'JRWK' reported that the tour party left London Victoria station en route for Newhaven and an overnight sea crossing to Dieppe. A ladies' trip to Ireland three years later departed from London Euston 'and with scarcely breathing time at Rugby, Crewe, Chester, and Bangor, steamed to Holyhead, where the "Lily" was in waiting to carry us over to Dublin' and then on to Killarney. The first Swiss party of 1890 left on Thursday 17 May at 8 pm from London, Liverpool Street station, visiting Antwerp, Brussels and Strasburg, and arriving in Lucerne on the Saturday evening. The starting point for a 'pioneer' journey to the Belgian Ardennes in 1891 also began at Liverpool Street, and used a steamer from Harwich in Essex to Antwerp in the Netherlands; while a Madeira itinerary (the same year) began at London Waterloo and set sail from Southampton. Harwich was also a departure point for steamships taking Polytechnic parties to Norway, as was Grimsby in 1897. The earliest surviving Polytechnic brochure, or 'Co-operative and Educational Holiday Tours – Programme of Special Tours' for 1895, reveals that Holborn Viaduct was the departure point for a Whitsuntide tour of Italy, leaving at 10 am on a Friday and arriving in Como the next day. A tourist wanting a week in Switzerland in that year could leave Britain with the Polytechnic most Fridays during the summer, arriving in Lucerne on the Saturday night.

Many of the themes of Polytechnic accounts of the outward journey appear in one of the earliest tour reports, 'RWK's article on that Easter 1887 trip to Paris. JRWK remembered the start of the trip like this:

At five minutes to eight o'clock on the night of Thursday, the 7th April, we left Victoria Station for Newhaven, which we reached, I think, somewhere about 10.30. Very few berths were secured, owing to the great number of passengers sailing, so we made ourselves as comfortable as possible, and left the harbour about ten minutes to two o'clock. The moon was shining serenely, but it must be confessed the channel was decidedly choppy, as some knew to their sorrow. Dieppe was reached, if I remember rightly, about nine o'clock, and after some hasty refreshment at the buffet, we took train for Paris, catching a glimpse of Rouen cathedral on our way. We arrived at Paris exactly at 1.15, presenting, after the effects of travel and mal de mer, rather a seedy appearance, which speedily vanished after some ablutions.

Polytechnic travel accounts tended to take a slightly euphemistic approach to seasickness. BALLYHOOLEY's article on another Paris trip the following year averred that 'One or two of us wished we were anywhere but on the rolling deep'. An uncredited author who joined the voyage to Majorca in August 1890 confided: 'Several fellow-voyageurs informed me in sepulchral tones that they had a "touch of indigestion".' Of the 195 passengers on a Baltic cruise in 1899, WGL wryly observed that 'only about twenty-five concerned themselves very much about the weather. Breakfast was considered unnecessary, luncheon was declined, and dinner was declared unsavoury except for a few thorough-going sailors in our party'.

The Polytechnic was keen to ensure that customer word of mouth on the holidays, including the journeys to the ultimate destination, was as positive as possible. To this end it reproduced in its 1897 brochure an article by Marianne Farningham, which had been published the previous August in the *Christian World*. Ms Farningham pointed out what she perceived as the healthy aspects of sea travel, while acknowledging the potential drawbacks:

> *A trip to Norway is especially good for tired brain-workers. Telegrams, letters, and newspapers can seldom assail those who travel by water, and life on the upper deck of the steamer is more soothing than exciting, while the fresh, bracing breezes, which blow all day long, induce sleep in the only natural way. Of course, the idea of crossing the North Sea is not always pleasant, but when the skies are blue, the breezes propitious, and the sea is calm, as was the case when the Polytechnic boat, the Ceylon, made its last voyage, even that part of the holiday is delightful.*

Sometimes it was not the weather (and sea) conditions which annoyed Polytechnic travellers so much as the perception that they were being short-changed, or even ripped off. Another unnamed writer told the following sorry tale of his party's time on board the *Prince Henriette*, a Belgian state mail boat that was conveying passengers from Dover to Ostend in September 1888:

> *This vessel has an upper and lower deck, the floor of the former completely covering the latter, as the party found to its cost. The commencement of the voyage was all right, singing and joking being the order of the day and the nice upper deck giving complete satisfaction. The drawback came when the ticket-collector came for his fares: "Second-class down below, gentlemen." It was no use to argue the point, and downstairs they went. The fares were paid; in fact overpaid, the cashier actually allowing the foreigner to charge a franc in excess. This, however, was afterwards refunded.*

Despite the occasional trying circumstances, Polytechnic parties generally found ways to keep their spirits up. One author observed, on an 1890 journey to Ireland, that 'most of the Poly boys, indifferent to the weather, got as near to Ireland as they could by gathering forward in a bunch with the look-out man in the bows, with whom they soon became quite chummy.' The following year Percy Lindley was 'struck with the serviceable looking walking rig of my eleven. Tweed cricket caps, flannel shirts, a sprinkling of knickers, and nothing new or startling in "tourist suitings." Knapsacks, folded waterproofs, and big bags to send on, by way of baggage.' He reported that 'No one in the morning [after the steamer departed] was able to report he had been ill. We entered the River Scheldt with light hearts and large appetites.' The diversions on board, as Fred Heale described for an account of a Norway voyage, included '[u]pon the fore deck a waterproof bath, about 9ft by 6ft, [which] is prepared for us between six and seven am, and I can tell you there is a goodly muster for it'.

If they were on board ship on a Sunday, the tourists' day would also include at least one religious service, faithfully attended and recounted. Sydney Axford's article about another Madeira party of August 1890 captures the frivolous and the faithful aspects of the voyage, along with an example of Poly philanthropy:

[Saturday] *We are all thoroughly enjoying ourselves (with the exception of those that are ill aforesaid). Two of our ladies are rather queer; one has kept her cabin, but she is coming up this evening. Two of the fellows are also rather queer. The others are pretty jolly up to the present. Hill is thoroughly enjoying himself. We had the fiddles on the table to day, to keep the plates from wandering about, and there was rather a poor show up, both at breakfast and dinner. Have just had tea, and are watching the sun set. We find plenty to do, in reading, games at chess, dominoes, and other more frivolous games, and generally wind-up the evening with a concert. The officers say all the fun is our end of the ship, and we are going to have sports on Monday. They generally do not commence that sort of thing till they have left Madeira, but as we seem pretty jolly, fun is to commence Monday, when the band will play for the first time …*

Sunday morning. – We are now out of the Bay of Biscay, and it is much calmer: we are going very steadily. All our invalids have come up again smiling, and at the breakfast table there was quite a good muster. At half-past ten the bells rang for church, so we all trooped down to the saloon, where the table had a Union Jack draped over it, and the Rev Mr Grubb, a passenger, read the prayers; he gave us a nice little sermon, and we had three hymns, the minister being organist and preacher in one. We had a collection for the Seaman's Orphan Asylum. Had a very nice Sunday dinner to-day, roast fowl, roast mutton, and other joints, tarts, pastry, cheese, and dessert. We have a good many children on board, and all the invalids are up and taking an airing, and warming themselves in the sun. We expect to be at Lisbon at 9 o'clock to night but we do not expect to land till to-morrow morning, when I shall post this. We have two salvation captains on board, and they are having a service on the deck, nearly everyone joining in the singing; the Rev Mr Grubb spoke a few words, which I thought very nice of him, as he is Church of England.

On another occasion, an outbreak of Polytechnic singing, on a boat waiting to depart for France, received 'the plaudits of both the passengers and those on the quay'. The 'Second Annual Swiss party' of twenty-six day-school boys and nine Institute members, as RA Ward described it, arrived in Brussels 'and created some sensation marching from the station to the hotel'. The same tour leader and author also reported an incident on a separate holiday where the locals took the initiative:

At Bale Station there was a great number of people on their way to a schutzenfeste or rifle match. A squad of competitors, accompanied by their excellent brass band, occupied the next car to ours, and on the way each party alternately sang songs, and when they alighted at Nebikon they formed up, waved their hats, and with ringing cheers shouted "Vive l'Angleterre," to which our fellows replied in an equally hearty manner.

These little pieces of self-promotion neatly capture some Polytechnic groups' apparent high spirits, high self-esteem and wish to be seen as the centre of attention – themes to which we will return when examining reports of the holidays themselves. The fun occasionally took on elements of slapstick, as 'WW' recalled from a May 1890 journey from Holyhead to Ireland in heavy rain:

The deck of the steamer was very slippery indeed, and in spite of the smooth passage walking was barely possible, several on board unwillingly indulging in some graceful figure skating, chiefly in the horizontal position greatly contributing to the amusement of the lucky ones who managed to remain on end.

The frequency and length of comments on outward journeys diminished, and all but disappeared, by the turn of the century, possibly due to readers' familiarity with the subject by then, or because smoother voyages caused fewer incidents worthy of description. By 1901, an unnamed writer could pass over the sea-trip from Southampton to St Malo simply by remarking that 'Much to the satisfaction of all, Britannia ruled the waves'.

Not every Polytechnic traveller found the sea-bound part of the outward journey to be most worthy of note. Wilfred Bryant set out alone to Switzerland in May 1905, sailing from Dover to Calais and joining a larger party in Paris. 'O how glad I was to reach the journey's end,' he wrote home to his father. The boat trip was uneventful and Bryant congratulated himself as 'a splendid sailor'. The four-hour train transfer to Paris (departing at 1.50 am) was not so pleasant: 'a nasty journey – an old carriage through which the heavy rain leaked & the temperature was chill. I didn't – couldn't sleep – tho' I dozed …' After meeting 'two strange Liverpool men' for an early morning glass of milk in Paris and observing the 'streets … full of folk – the women hatless as usual', Bryant caught the 8.45 am to Basle along with others who had spent the night in the French capital. The train journey was more eventful than the Dover-Calais boat:

An incident occured at TROYES: for the brake of the carriage got wrong & we were all bundled out & I had been very comfortable by the open window & the whole side of the carriage was open to the air. The French officials made much ado before another carriage was linked on & the joining was considerably delayed. It was amusing at the boundary between FRANCE & GERMANY (i.e. ALSACE). The whole train was emptied & we had to cart our luggage through the Customs & after examination (I escaped opening mine throughout) we were penned up like sheep in a fold until the doors were unlocked & we could return to our carriage. It WAS a farce! & carrying a heavy bag worked up corns in my tender hands!

The food was not to his liking, either, and even the scenery disappointed Bryant, as he looked out eagerly for snowy mountains:

I lunched in the train & the affair took 1 ½ hours – for 4 wretched courses: the first dish was some "yellow" mess – the second veal & I finished with cherries. Great interest seemed to be taken in the train by the townsfolk we passed. I saw how often a shrine by the wayside & every village had its church spire as in England. But heavy rain fell again later & I entered SWITZERLAND under leaden skies. BALE is a large place but I do not think I saw the RHINE. We had to change again here – pass the Customs & hurry to the Swiss train. I was more tired than ever & the scenery was … more like the WYE valley – pretty peeks of wood-clothed hills but no snow mountains! In fact I have been terribly disappointed so far. Well – to cut a long story short we reached LUCERNE at last about 9 pm – in the pouring rain & darkness & sailed down the LAKE to the Chalets at SEEBURG.

Bryant's holiday improved from that point onwards (as we shall see later). Perhaps some company on the journey would have helped, as he acknowledged: 'I have felt very lonely & don't think it is worth it coming away alone. A companion is an absolute necessity for true enjoyment.'

Another traveller to Switzerland, Thomas Todrick, had taken the opposite approach to his travel arrangements a few years earlier, as he recounted to a Dundee publication *The People's Journal* – an article republished in the Polytechnic's 1897 brochure. Todrick travelled from Auchinclash via Edinburgh to London, to join the main party of forty 'Polytechnickers' at 'that mighty big station they call Victoria'. Having never been south of the Tweed before, Todrick recounted that:

> [I]*t was passing pleasant to listen to the sweet liquid tones of the English speech … Not a soul among them thought himself or herself better than his or her neighbour, and it was a company as joyous as old Chaucer's that flashed through the smiling hop-gardens and corn fields to Canterbury.*

Having survived the sea trip from Dover to Ostend, Todrick and his wife Peggy found themselves sitting down to dinner in Brussels – at which point a classic travel misunderstanding was lurking in ambush for him:

> *Horrificating tales had been told me about the traffic the Belgian butchers had in horse flesh, and that decayed nags from Scotland found their way in to the dining tables, and so I had a kind of a dwam when the "garsong" (that's the waiter) ask me to take some "horse daivers".*

"No, sir," said I, as sharply as I could, "I'll eat no horse flesh though I'm obligated to live on crowdie till I get back to Scotland."

Everybody snickered and laughed but Peggy, who reddened like a Kilmarnock cowl, and I was real mad at myself, when Mrs Brewster, being a good French scholar, and a German one likewise, whispered to me that "horse daivers" was French for appeteezers. I took a big draucht of a nice caller beer they called Kokelberg, and so swallowed my shame; but I must needs add that the viands we got were wholesome and bonnily cooked, and as a baker myself I'm in manner bound to praise the loaf brad they sat before us.

Apart from another brief misunderstanding about the need to adjust his watch for Continental time, Todrick experienced no further misfortunes on his way to Lucerne.

Frequently the interim stops along the way to Lucerne or other Continental destinations involved little more than a dash around the main tourist sights and brief refreshment. For some groups, more time was available and their activities were less conventional. A group of plumbers on their way to the 1889 Paris Exposition took the opportunity to research the standard of French workmanship in their own professional area at Rouen station. They were not impressed:

[W]e *discovered … some arrangements which we at once pronounced to be unsanitary, not because of any defect in the apparatus, but rather on account of the entire absence of anything to which such a term could be applied… while the apparatus was being made, the people had made use of the apartment without waiting for the plumbers to finish their work. Our first impressions were consequently rather unfavourable, if not of the plumbing, certainly of the habits of the people.*

'Three Poly boys' who took a fortnight's tour of Germany, France, and Switzerland eight years later formed similarly less than positive conclusions of Cologne,

whose cathedral spires at once arrested the attention of our adventurers; then a stroll round the town and a swim in the magnificent baths. After tea the bikes are brought into such action as the railway officials have left them capable of, and

a smooth run of twenty miles is made to Bonn, the way out of Cologne giving us
views of the Bridge of Boats across the Rhine. There is a reason for everything,
and the reason for Eau de Cologne is as plain as a pikestaff once you have been
through the "city of 100 smells."

Bonn on the other hand 'with its university, its beer gardens, its lovely walks, and flower-bedecked villas, is a place to dream in, and live in too, for mine host only charged us five marks for bed and breakfast, which works out at 1s 8d per head'.

Like many of their fellow Polytechnic tourists over the years, the 'Poly boys' accepted the downsides of the long outward journey, while enjoying the experience overall. In the next chapter we'll take a look at what the tourists did, once they had reached their ultimate holiday destination.

Chapter 6

Being There: What the Tourists Did

Polytechnic holidays came, as we have seen, in various shapes and sizes. The institution's London location made day trips to northern continental Europe possible, especially France. The most popular Poly holidays, to Switzerland and in particular Lucerne, typically involved staying a week in that city. Tourists with a little more time and money at their disposal could travel on to southern Europe, with Italy offering many possibilities. Or, in the early years of the PTA, they could go north and east from Britain, cruising and walking around Norway and other parts of Scandinavia.

If a Polytechnic tourist wanted to stay in the British Isles (or if economic circumstances dictated it), the network of holiday homes in south-eastern England, the south-west and other locations was available. If he or she still wanted the feeling of crossing a border, Scotland, Ireland and the Isle of Man awaited.

The location, and the duration of a holiday, clearly influenced what the tourists got up to, once they had arrived, as this chapter will show. Those with relatively deep pockets and a lot of free time could venture to the Holy Land or even to the USA, for a month or more. However, apart from the letters of Quintin Hogg and his wife, travel accounts published in *Home Tidings*, later the *Polytechnic Magazine*, tended to focus on continental Europe and on holidays within the British Isles. It is these accounts, along with the letters of Wilfred Bryant's 1905 Swiss trip, on which this chapter is based.

Not surprisingly, the short day trips across the Channel had a certain frantic quality to them, with the holidaymakers striving to make every moment count. An August 1888 excursion to Boulogne flashed by, if the report of 'ONE WHO WENT' is accurate:

> *Passing along the quay we went on to the Rue Grand and visited the Museum. Some of the pictures here called forth admiration. Shortly after … we went*

through the fair ground to Rue de Calais. Having arranged the preliminaries we were soon partaking of a good repast. Now came a little fun. The 'Change being closed we had to go on as best we could, and passed on up Rue de Calais to the Colonne. Here 265 steps tempted the venturers to a view from the summit, and, having provided lanterns, we ascended, and were well paid for our trouble. Returning to terra firma we went round by the cliff to Boulogne, near the Casino, visiting the Cathedral of Notre Dame de Boulogne en route. Then home to tea, which we thoroughly enjoyed, tea and coffee being provided ad libitum. Making our farewells we were about to pass on again; but, alas! he who has not had the trouble of collecting thirteen fellows together knows little of what followed. Some at one shop, some at another, only to be missing a few minutes later; while some were buying handkerchiefs, others visiting museums – all seeking a "souvenir" of the place. At last we started for the circus, but, alas, half an hour late, only to find all the seats taken; so we journeyed to the Casino and watched things there. Taking a walk round the place we at last determined to go out to the Sportsman Café on the quay. It was raining fast, but we managed to get there pretty soon. Here we stayed chaffing and laughing until 1.30 am, when we left to catch our boat. We soon got scattered in the darkness on account of the effluvia so plentiful here at night.

Eleven years later, the Polytechnic Ramblers paid a short visit to Boulogne – albeit with a couple of members on their way back from a longer stay in Switzerland and Italy. An early morning swim and a look at the cathedral and the local dungeons preceded a visit to a pen and pencil-case works an Englishman managed. The real drama of the holiday took place on the return train journey when severe delays meant that at Tonbridge, as Alf Bailey gleefully reported:

[T]he refreshment room was besieged by two or three hundred people, and an awful scuffle ensued over half a pork pie, which luckily had been forgotten and left on the counter all by itself. Hurray! The Poly came in first as usual, as that half pork pie was captured by our team and borne in triumph to our railway carriage, and there it disappeared.

Even in a light-hearted way, this vignette depicted the tour as a success story. No doubt this reflected the overall view of the Polytechnic by its leadership, members and students who remembered at all times that it was the first and largest institution of its type in the land. But, we shall return to the theme of travel accounts depicting Polytechnic success stories later.

The longer journeys to Switzerland and beyond inevitably included brief stops along the way. These, too, were an opportunity to clock up some local sightseeing. Robert Avey Ward told readers that one of the Swiss expeditions that he led arrived one morning in Brussels: 'During a three hours' stroll we managed to see the Cathedral, the New Museum, the Law Courts, and Hotel de Ville, to say nothing of smaller sights.' The party also took its chance to look round Basle (or Bale, as the articles commonly spelt it), finding St Jacob's Monument, the town hall and 'some of the churches'. In 1895 (over fifty years before Ian Fleming decided to purloin the initial for the *nom de plume* of James Bond's boss), 'M' gave the *Polytechnic Magazine* a detailed article on visits to various cities, including some capitals, en route to Lucerne by a tour party punningly called 'The "Capitalists" of Europe'. The itinerary included Brussels, Amsterdam, Hanover, Berlin, Dresden, Vienna and Munich. 'All the arrangements,' remarked 'M' with satisfaction, 'were thorough, but not too rigid, and carried out with admirable tact by our accomplished leader and his amiable mother'. The tour leader's conscientious approach delighted 'M':

Of course, we carried with us many of our own ways of doing, to the no small astonishment of the foreigners. For instance, our leader had a natural anxiety that none of his party should go astray, so when he thought there was some danger of that, he blew a blast upon a whistle! It proved too much for the official mind in Berlin, where a policeman was nearly thrown into a fit at the sound, and directed that it was never to be done again, a command more honoured in the breach than in the observance.

Things were less frenetic at the PTA's main base – its chaléts in Lucerne. The attractions of a Poly holiday here were manifold. The chalets themselves were a secure, known quantity in a location where the tourists could relax and mingle with their fellow guests. The lake and its surrounding features, including mountains, offered an accessible set of adventures, within easy reach. Wilfred Bryant told his father that 'the original buildings were formerly a monastery & then passed to an artist's hands: whether the fine old furniture & armour &

pictures & statuary belonged to the monks or the artist or were purchased by Mr Mitchell I have not yet discovered'. (In fact Mitchell had made a number of astute second-hand buys soon after securing the chalets for the Polytechnic.)

Many tours arrived on a Saturday night, enabling tourists to spend the Sunday resting and acclimatising. Again Robery Avey Ward gives a vivid summary:

> *Lucerne was reached at 5.40, and we at once proceeded to the hotel, and afterwards a few of us had a walk by the beautiful lake in the starlight. The next day was Sunday. We went to the English Church in the morning, and listened to an excellent sermon; then having a walk by the lake with its peculiar green water, with gardens down to the banks, and round us the mountains extending, as we faced the lake, from the Rigi on the left to Mount Pilatus on the right. We visited the Lion* [a famous statue], *by Thorwaldsen, and saw most of Lucerne in the day, leaving it early the next morning by steamboat, a magnificent panorama opening at each bend, passing the Rigi railway with its comical skew* [of] *locomotives and cars, Schiller's monument, the Axenstrasse, a tunnel cut in the rock, lighted by arches abutting on the lake, past Tells Platte, where the patriot is said to have escaped by leaping from the boat; the Fluhlen, the other end of the lake from Lucerne. Here we disembarked, and a sharp walk of forty minutes brought us to Altorf, where we saw the statue of Tell, and the fountain marking the spots where the shooting is said to have occurred. We rode by train to Amsteg, and after lunch started to walk to Andermatt, the road traversing the valley of the Reuss, through beautiful scenery, snow clad peaks, waterfalls, and the rushing river. We passed Goschenen and the entrance to the St Gotthard main tunnel, then climbed the road and reached the Devil's Bridge, spanning the river at a great height, just below a magnificent waterfall over rugged rocks. Then on again, till emerging from a tunnel, the lights of Andermatt, pretty, dirty Andermatt, showed close ahead, giving new ardour to the most fatigued, and bringing a ringing cheer from the boys. We were soon in the hotel, dined, and went to bed. The next day (Tuesday) was a soaker, and most of us stayed in all day, though some went back to see the Devil's Bridge in the daylight. That night we had a concert in the coffee-room, songs and recitations abounding ...*

On occasions, weather permitting, the Sunday service took place in the open air. Bryant recorded that 'In this Canton there is a strict law against services of all kinds in the open air but the Polytechnic have secured the single & therefore signal advantage of being able to do so'.

The Lucerne tours Ward led, which seem to have consisted primarily of boys from the day school but with some members as well, used a restful Sunday as a launching pad for visits to sites of historical interest (such as the monument to Schiller and the statue of William Tell, as described above) and geological interest, namely waterfalls, glaciers and mountains. The groups reached some of these landmarks by steamboat and others on extended walks, which took several days, staying at various hotels along the way. Here is Ward's description of events on 27–28 July 1889:

During breakfast … it came on to snow, and we started in a blinding cutting snowstorm, changing to rain, or rather we cut our way through the raincloud in single file, crossing the Rider Alo, and reaching the hotel of that name about midday, where hot coffee provided a welcome stimulant. Then began the descent by the worst path imaginable, rocky, stony, slippy, and jolty, till, as one member put it, every organ in our bodies had been jolted into a new place, and our knees became double-jointed. Glad, very, were we when we reached level ground again and pegged on to Brigne. This is a peculiar old-fashioned place at the Swiss end of the Simplon Pass, the architecture of many of the buildings being distinctly Moorish, while the church and hospital have metal cupolas. We left Brigne on Sunday morning, 28th, and walked leisurely on to Visp along a novelty to us, a broad flat road, then started along the valley of the Visp by a winding, rocky, insect-infected path. At three we halted, and in a shady place by the roadside had our Sunday service of hymns, bible reading, and a short address; then on again through Stalden, a village where no two houses are on the same level, and the high street cannot be climbed except by men and mules, as a wagon, however strong, couldn't stand it. Here we turned sharp to the right, along a new valley for miles and miles, till at 8 o'clock St Nicholas was reached, and dinner and bed was eagerly sought for. Still in the same valley we pushed on the next morning, but over much better roads, halting at the foot of the Weisshorn, with its beautiful glacier, while ahead of us up the valley was Monte Rosa, one mass of snow and the Breithorn. On again past rills, brooks, and cascades falling into the river below, till turning a corner the Matterhorn came suddenly into sight, a towering mass of bare rock nearly 15,000 feet high. It was a beautiful sight, and this first glimpse will be always remembered by many besides myself. On again till Zermatt, with its letters from home, the first since we had started, was reached, and happy were those with news, and to hear, I am thankful to say, in every case all was well at home.

The combination of walking, climbing and in some cases 'slipping, sliding and jolting' continued for another week, before Ward's party began the long journey back to London.

As a single man visiting with, but not as a close part of, a Polytechnic party sixteen years later, Wilfred Bryant's record of his time in Lucerne is, not surprisingly, a little different – and he was more at liberty to set his own itinerary. His letters focused initially on the frustration of unending rain, which hid the mountains from view and which caused him to opt out of an excursion to Mount Rigi. Bryant passed the time, among other things, by visiting the English cemetery high above the town: 'Graves are numerous already & many are sad. One unmarked is that of a young couple on their honeymoon drowned in the Lake last year!' When not writing letters in the evenings, Bryant got to know other holidaymakers, by talking and dancing with them. As the bad weather continued, Bryant lost patience, booking a trip to the Rhine Falls:

At first sight they seem as nothing & indeed the actual fall is insignificant but it is when you stand actually midway at their side that the stupendous volume of water – seething, chaotic – whirling, foaming, tumbling … Tis altogether a difference experience to TROLLMATTAN & as a tumbling mass far finer but the Swedish Fall is a grand cataract. From the grounds of Castle Laufen the chief views are obtained & there is a boat holding tea – we were most cleverly ferried across almost at the very foot of the FALLS. The way in which the skilled boatman watched the currents was the finest bit of work I have ever seen. He brought us exactly to the point opposite in spite of the current! I put my hand in the RHINE waters! Then we lunched in the Hotel Bellevue & returned by train to ZURICH the largest town in Switzerland, which I rapidly surveyed alone in an hour. A gleam of sunshine … the glories of LAKES ZURICH & ZUG [and] visible the snow-clad ALPS & "O the difference to me." The contrast of the same scene as I saw it in the rain gloom of the morning & the sunshine of the afternoon was indescribable.

From that point, the weather and Bryant's outlook became sunnier. He admired the railways and the 'magnificence' of the local churches; and he achieved the 'conquest' (a revealing word) of Mount Pilatus on a brilliantly sunny day. Bryant also made the acquaintance of two ladies 'from the Shepherd's Bush district'. With them he explored Stanstaad and they 'walked through the hot noontide down the flower-strewn valley floor … to BUOCHS where the AAR enters the Lake. Here we had lunch like lotus-eaters on the balcony of the Hotel Lausanne'. The trio ascended Mount Rigi, with another (unnamed) woman the following day and it seems Bryant had fallen in love with more than just the scenery:

I saw everything to perfection. We walked down half the way back – a glorious experience – with the Lake & Lucerne at our feet & I visited the Shepherds' Church & drank of the Holy Well. How clean & cool & adorned the Swiss churches are even in the out-of-the-way valleys! So exhausted were we with our RIGI exploit that when we returned Miss Lewis Miss Cartwright & I – all hatted – had a charming starlit walk up into the woods – past the English cemetery & on towards MEGGEN: but we lost our way & wandered by lane & meadow until we recovered the road & didn't get back till after 10 pm.

Yesterday & today I have spent in their company & you wouldn't know me for my youthfulness. Their young enthusiasms are like a tonic on my 'aged' pessimism! On the boat coming back from RIGI my four lady friends & I cried our eyes out with laughing. I told them a lot of my yarns – like the story of William Stickers: & whether referring to us or not, somebody was heard to remark "What strange people one does meet abroad!" Our merry party at the stern of the boat amused the German & Swiss onlookers immensely.

The ladies departed for home before Bryant, leaving him 'friendless' to witness a near-accident as three parties climbed 3,000 feet above Grindelwald, as a lady lost her footing and fell, '[d]ragging with her another lady & a heavy middle-aged man as well as the guide himself! They were pulled up in time, however, by the rest of their party, else there was a nasty crevasse … the haunches and hands of those who fell were badly skinned.'

Despite the early departure of his new-found friends, and this almost fatal incident, Bryant clearly enjoyed his holiday a great deal. He returned to Lucerne in 1909 – on that occasion with his new wife.

Although they lacked the still calm centre that Lucerne provided for the Polytechnic's Swiss holidays, its Norwegian tours were also extremely popular and the subject of many reports back to students and members through the *Polytechnic Magazine*. Often these tours' first port of call within Norway was at Stavanger, where those members of the party suffering from seasickness could recover in anticipation of the exertions to come. This provided the chance to see the town's sights, as 'THE PASSENGER WHO ENJOYED IT THE MOST' recalled in 1891: 'The observatory tower, the cathedral, with its quaint pulpit and memorial tablets, the pleasure gardens at Bergsted, were in turn visited, and after breakfast … the Belvedere on Vaalandspiben from whence an excellent view was obtained.' The boat would then carry its tourists through fjords and past islands, reaching the Folgefond glacier where the braver souls prepared to make the crossing on foot:

> *At one am on the morning of the 19th August, the* SS Fridtjof, *lying at the head of the Mauranger fjord, looked more like an abode of the forty thieves than a respectable boat carrying the fifth Norway Polytechnic party. Our energetic friend Hill was going round to some twenty-six of our berths with a dim lantern, muttering low, "Now for the Folgefond – ten minutes to dress; keep quiet." Everything had been prepared over night – the strongest boots looked out, socks well soaped, and macintosh strapped ready for the shoulders. The Folgefonders were soon on deck, and there found a long table ready spread, lighted apparently by the same dim lantern, and well supplied with meat, eggs, and coffee. After a rapid meal, each of us was given a packet of food for the expedition, and then, when all was ready, we stood for prayer. As we stood there under the light of the stars, with the lake hundreds of feet deep beneath us, and the black mass of the mountains all but closing us in, Mr Manton Smith, in his splendid, clear voice commended us to the care of our protecting God …*

Despite one or two near misses, and occasional challenges such as the lack of provisions or even sledges for the crossings, invariably the reports proclaimed these expeditions to be a complete success. They might have been nerve-wracking nonetheless: on one occasion, 'a special thanksgiving service was held on board in commemoration of all arriving home safe'. As a less perilous alternative, the tourists also had the chance to sit in a *stolkjarre* (a one-horse carriage on two wheels) driven by a local, as it passed waterfalls and other sights. If this happened in the late evening, the scenery left an indelible impression upon the memory of those who experienced it – as did the occasional surprise upon arrival at the next stop:

> *Stalheim was reached just about 4 o'clock, and here the finest hotel in Norway has just been completed. On the arrival of the advance guard they detected the smell of burning, and Mr Mitchell, with a few others, made a detour of the premises, the inmates of which were all asleep, and presently found that a fire had broken out in the bakery. An alarm was given, and the fire was soon extinguished. The visitors all turned out more alarmed, perhaps, at the invasion than at the fire.*

Meanwhile, on-board activities included board games such as deck billiards and even a cock-fighting competition, as a Dr R Marshall recalled from a 1903 cruise. Invariably the holiday ended with a vote of thanks to the captain and crew and to the tour leaders and organisers, who accepted presentations of glass claret jugs, cigarette cases and other desirable items.

Perhaps the most vivid incident of all the Norway cruises occurred in 1891, with the Polytechnic boat nearing Odde and Robert Mitchell on the scene. What followed according to Mitchell may have been the precursor of every anecdote and advertisement we have ever heard or read about the rivalry of Britain and Germany – except that, in this case, no towels or beaches came into it:

> *We arrived at Odde at about 10 o'clock. Here we had a most interesting and exciting incident. When about three miles from Odde I saw, in the distance, three large vessels coming up to us at full steam. We soon discovered it was the German Emperor's yacht, and two men-of-war accompanying him. I at once felt all hope was gone of our getting any conveyance for the Lotefos Waterfall, and for a time hardly knew what to do. However, I got the captain to send orders to the engineer to put on as much steam as possible, so as to arrive at Odde before the Imperial yacht was sighted. This was done, and with the utmost despatch I got ashore; before the yacht had turned the point I had engaged every conveyance in the place, though I had to pay a good deal extra. I got the passengers down with as much speed as possible, and had about half of them accommodated when the Imperial boats hove in sight. Then there was a scene of excitement. The horses*

were wanted to be retained, but having engaged them of course I refused, as it was a case of then or never for our party. We all got off just as the Hohenzollern anchored and an order was sent on shore for twenty horses, but there was not a single one left. A courier was despatched after us by the hotel proprietor, but we had arrived at the falls before we were overtaken, and on our way home we met the German party doing the journey on foot, the Emperor having stayed on board. As we were leaving we steamed alongside the yacht, the whole party singing the "Watch on the Rhine," and we fired off our four guns as a salute. The Emperor came forward and saluted our party, whereupon, in the most innocent fashion everybody started singing "For He's a Jolly Good Fellow." The Emperor joined with the officers on board in laughing heartily at the sentiments of the song. Our own national anthem followed, and after the Imperial yacht had saluted us we steamed off.

As Quintin Hogg remarked, 'It is not often ordinary folk have a chance of getting to the windward side of an emperor, but sooner or later we generally manage to do *most* things at the Poly.'

No doubt this blend of humour, adventure and a triumph over an international rival went down well back in Regent Street. It certainly wasn't the only travel account that played upon teasing hints of militarism and patriotism. Percy Lindley's report on a 'pioneer' trip (i.e. the first organised by the Polytechnic) to the Ardennes, also in 1891, traded heavily on such tropes. Consider, for example, his description of the appointment of an assistant tour leader:

[At Antwerp] a quartermaster was formally appointed. Part of his duties were to assist me with the disbursements, and to debit each fellow with his share of incidentals and extras. Devoted quartermaster! I see the gay twinkle in his blue eye when he started with this first lot of twopences in a currency he did not understand. And I recall later the pensive far-away look on his face at the end of a day's march, when we had all been seized with a quenchless thirst, and the ten, and fifteen, and twenty centimes drinks, of milk, and soda, and coffee, and beer, chased each other through his tired brain.

The party went on to Waterloo where 'with the comfortable Hotel du Musee in the centre of the Field as our headquarters, fought the battle over again and were photographed under the shot-scarred walls of Hougoumont.' Then came an exhausting walk to Rochefort:

> *Next morning we started for Rochefort, a walk of thirty odd miles, with plenty of wading and rock climbing and forest clambering in the Less Valley. None but English and lunatics go this way to Rochefort. The narrow tracks are overgrown with bramble, briar, beech, and hazel. Now the way lies close by the rocky stream, now it ascends a hundred feet above. Here and there a mass of rock blocks the way, and one has to wade to one's middle through the river. At last, as the sun was setting, we came out at the village of Houyet to welcome coffee and bread and butter. We feel we have earned our lunch. Dinner is waiting at Rochefort. We learn that Rochefort is four good hours' walk further on. If we step out we should be there by midnight. A steep climb up a winding mountain road, skirting dark woods and misty valleys, out into high open country, down again as the shadows deeper, into another valley. Something ahead looks like a pole standing against some rising ground. It is a perfectly straight road. Are we all right? We look at map and compass by match light. Yes, that's the road. By the end of an hour we have had enough of it. Cross roads at last by way of diversion. Somebody climb the sign post, with the matches. Rochefort to the left, 12 kilometres. We have only another 7½ miles, and it is 10 o'clock. But we wish Rochefort would send out the dinner to meet us. The villages are fast asleep, and we would give something for a veal cutlet. Two pairs of knickerbockers make the pace, and we swing along to choruses sung in quick march time. Then we hear the trickle of water on the road side, and the twelve pioneers are lying flat on the ground with their heads over the water. It would make a noble subject for a flash-light photograph.*

This is not to say that the holidays totally omitted the element of education, which had been so important in the origins of the tours. The presence of geologists on Norwegian cruises and guest speakers (such as Professor Spadoni who took a Poly party on a tour of ancient Rome at Christmas 1894) was a reminder that the tourists should also be ready to learn. As late as 1902, Arthur W Wright could tell readers that the group touring north-eastern France under the leadership of Louis Graveline (a French tutor at the Polytechnic) had visited an exhibition in Lille, 'one of the great manufacturing towns of France [especially] the cotton-spinning industry.' Even in the accounts quoted above, the emphasis was rarely on unbridled fun. Praising a Madeira tour in the *Polytechnic Magazine*'s letters section, Kate Stevens noted that "What struck me most was the high moral turn pervading the party, and with what ease and naturalness the conversation often took a deeper turn.' Nonetheless, Polytechnic tourists clearly had what one correspondent called 'a capacity for enjoyment', which pervaded the image of the holidays they conveyed back home.

Many of the same themes come through in the reports of Polytechnic holidays within the British Isles. Perhaps the longest journeys involved leaving London Euston on the train for Holyhead, via Rugby, Crewe, Chester and Bangor. From Holyhead, a boat would carry the tourists across the Irish Sea, using Dublin as a brief stopping point on their way to Killarney. The tours left London on a Friday evening, arriving in Killarney on the following evening. As with some of the continental tours, this schedule enabled Sunday to be a day of rest and worship interspersed with some walks before, as one correspondent put it, the 'real working pleasure of our stay here began'.

For many this was fishing (particularly for trout), swimming and bathing, although we should remember that the majority of Polytechnic members and students, and authors of travel accounts in the inhouse magazine were male. What did the lady members of a tour party pass the time?

Fortunately, we can gain at least a glimpse of the answer to that question from the contents of two letters in the Sisters' Institute section of the *Polytechnic Magazine* (6 June 1890) about a stay in 'Old Ireland', as the unnamed writer of the first, longer letter called it. For her, the outward journey seems to have been one long exercise in not rising to provocation:

> [While] *mak*[ing] *ourselves presentable* [at Dublin] … *some of the great unwashed (not so particular about appearances) kindly disposed of the breakfast prepared for us … Mr Bird and Mr Axford very kindly looked after our luggage for us, and enjoyed themselves by trying to frighten us with accounts of the dreadful weather they had experienced. But our serenity was undisturbed, for we had made arrangements with the Clerk of the Weather, which have been pretty faithfully carried out …*

After attending church on Sunday morning, the ladies took a guided walk into the Gap of Dunloe, where echoes of visitors' voices were nicknamed Paddy

Blake, 'a schoolmaster who came to a bad end through infringing on a woman's prerogative of having the last word in matrimonial disputes' and who hence 'makes a point of always agreeing with the last sentiment uttered'.

The 'real business' (to quote an earlier correspondent) was to begin on the following Wednesday when, 'In spite of all advice and warning to the contrary, we decided to tackle Carrantuohill … we started off in the best of spirits, hoping to show that we are ripe for a Swiss trip.' In other words, the gentler mountain ascents of Ireland might be a proving ground for the female tourists in the party to prove their worth:

Nor were we disappointed, for all the eleven who started reached the top without drawing much upon Dan's help. We thoroughly enjoyed the ascent, as we took it in easy stages, climbing a little and then stopping to admire the views which became wider and grander as we got higher. Upon reaching the top we… settled down to drink in the beauty and sublimity of the scene. The day being so remarkably clear we could see for about fifty miles around. We were surrounded by range upon range of grand old mountains, rising massive and mighty one beyond the other. Here and there were lovely, deep-blue mountain lakes dotted with picturesque islands, while away in the distance stretched the silver sea. Altogether the panorama before us was quite awe inspiring, and such as we shall never forget. Before descending we christened the highest well in Ireland after ourselves. Dan has faithfully promised to point out "The Maiden's Well" to all whom he conducts. Mr Moriarty was pleased to compliment us on our pluck, "though I says it as shouldn't," and seemed quite proud of us. Nor were we without a certain glow of satisfaction at having performed what had been pointed out as an impossibility. The exhilarating influence of the mountain air more than repaid us for our pains. The scorching sun soon played sad havoc with some of our complexions, but for that we care not. While we were conquering Carrantuohill, the rest spent the day in another direction, and climbed what we very condescendingly called a "mole hill" …

The rest of the week passed with drives in the countryside and, on Saturday, a visit to the weekly market and monthly pig fair in Killarney. The ladies spent the day wandering round the town 'studying the people' – not an activity many male-written accounts mentioned.

Study of a more formal type was one part of the tours being organised at around this time in Scotland. The parties departed London from King's Cross, going through Berwick as their train crossed the border and made for Edinburgh. From the Scottish capital, the group split into sub-sections, with some taking a steamboat down the Clyde to Glasgow, while others went to North Berwick. One of the most popular excursions was to view the Forth Bridge, with some Polytechnic holidaymakers able to compare it with the Eiffel Tower which they had seen in Paris in 1889. But, perhaps the most unusual excursion – at least to twenty-first century eyes – was a trip to a coal mine at Dysart, owned by Lord Rosslyn with whom the tour organisers had agreed the event. JW Minister described the day thus:

Mr Patterson, the Manager, met us at the station and first showed us the works above ground. We then came to the shaft; this was scarcely five feet square, and dropped straight down lowered, an overseer and three of the party entered the cap and at a word to the engineman quickly descended. The cap then came up for more, and so on, till the whole party were below. The rapidity of the descent is rather startling, but once below that is soon forgotten. The mine is a self-ventilating one, and the air which finds its way into it is wonderfully pure. Fire damp is unknown, and naked lamps are used with perfect safety. The miners work 8 hours a day (from 6 am till 2) and about 300 tons of coal are brought up daily, 3000 tons of water being pumped up in the same period. Arrived below, we each arm ourselves with a lamp and begin peering around. Floor, sides, and ceiling, all consist of coal, and preceded and followed by an overseer with Mr Patterson to explain, we make a tour of the mine, scrambling over lumps of coal and dodging the streams and pools of jet black water lying seductively in our path. We first reach the stables and presently stand back off the rails as a horse, dragging a train of trucks after him, slowly passes a boy sitting on one of the trucks, with lamp fastened to cap and eyes glittering, looking more like an imp than a human being. We next proceed to the working face of the mine, and see the men picking the coal; jogging on we ultimately go half a mile under the sea, being as far beneath the Forth as the top of the Forth Bridge is above it. At the next halt some go down a few hundred feet deeper to see the pump, a beautiful and ingenious piece of machinery, but most of us prefer daylight, so make our way to the nearest shaft, and entering the cap are brought to the surface in a twinkling.

We divest ourselves of as much dirt as possible, and await the others, and when all have washed, Mr. Patterson conducts us through the grounds of Lord Rosslyn's house to the town, where we thank him and say goodbye. The experience was a striking one, and the weird strangeness of the place will no doubt cling to the memory of every member of the party.

While trips to coal mines may well have historical interest today, this was more in the nature of professional development or education at that time. No doubt the next outing to the Trossachs, climbing 800 feet up the side of Craigmore, through the pass of Aberfoyle, was appreciated all the more for the 'pure mountain air [which] rushed thrilling into our lungs'. Further days out visited Loch Lomond and Loch Long, with a twenty-four-mile sailing trip, which called at Dunoon and Greenock before the party met a train to take them back to Edinburgh.

Of course, as we have seen, holidaymakers did not have to travel so far for a holiday with the Polytechnic. They could stay at a holiday home in Clacton on Sea, hosted by Mr and Mrs Deas, and enjoy a week of 'rowing, fishing, bathing and yachting'. One 1891 holidaymaker recalled that 200 oysters were caught at Brightlingsea, and that the Poly parties even found time to beat local teams in games of cricket and tennis. Several joined a temperance parade at Colchester, while evenings passed in a succession of singsongs by the piano. Finally, the group 'sorrowfully left Clacton Pier amidst the waving of handkerchiefs from the girls we had left behind us.' Around the other side of London, West Cliff House in Ramsgate was another Poly holiday home, which Robert Mitchell's wife Isabella hosted (on those rare occasions when she was not based in Lucerne). Highlights of the stay at West Cliff House included drives through St Lawrence, Sandwich, Birchington and Canterbury including the cathedral. 'Special arrangements were also made at reduced fares for the conveyance of our various parties on short yachting tours round the bay', wrote 'ONE OF THE PARTY' about the visit of forty members of the Sisters Institute in September 1891, and lawn croquet and strolls around the local hayfields were 'of great amusement to many of the party'.

Perhaps surprisingly, given its use of Scotland and Ireland for holidays, the Polytechnic and the emerging PTA do not seem to have had any holiday homes in Wales. They did make it as far west as Weston-super-Mare in 1894, at Lewisham House. WM Edgar and four other co-signatories on a letter attested that:

The hills (and the neighbourhood is all hills) are wooded to their summits, and the most pleasant walks and drives imaginable are to be found in their cool secluded valleys. Who has not heard of Lorna Doone and honest John Ridd. Here we are on the very borders of their country – the coombs and valleys, the waterfalls and cliffs, vieing with Norway in picturesque beauty.

The house acted as a base for excursions in the surrounding countryside. There was even the chance to join in local sports from time to time as 'A BOROUGH POLYITE' (a revealingly suburban *nom de plume* hinting at the reach of the Polytechnic in terms of its clientele) reported:

The day spent at Cheddar will linger long in the memory of all. The Weston CC having challenged the visitors, our fellows were invited to furnish five players for the visitors. The match was played on Wednesday, and although we were on the defeated side, we were by no means disgraced. Having to bat first the visitors compiled 65, of which number Stanley made 20, and Slous 17 not out. Both played excellent cricket. In the venture of the Weston eleven, they made 105. Albert Gray bowled splendidly, taking 7 wickets for 43.

Poly tourists could go by steamer to Lynmouth, Ilfracombe, Wadda Bay, Clovelly and places on the Welsh coast. Or they could take the train to Glastonbury, Tintern Abbey and other places of historic interest.

By the end of the century the Isle of Man, or 'Manxland' as one writer called it, also hosted a Poly holiday home. Tennis, croquet and yachting all held the tourists' attention, as did other attractions such as Snaefell and the town of Peel – and there was even the odd trip to Northern Ireland. The Poly base was Milntown House, which Charles Fells Latham labelled as a 'Polytechnic paradise':

It is a fine old-world country mansion dating from times when "an Englishman's (or Manxman's) house was his castle." Parts have been rebuilt (in 1830) by Deemster Christian, but all the old features are preserved. The old oak doors are from the earlier building, and are said to be from a Spanish galleon wrecked after the Armada. The approach is by a handsome avenue of trees, leading to the main entrance. The entrance hall is a fine key-note to the glories of the place.

Carried the whole height of the building, it has a gallery two sides, and access to the innumerable picturesque rooms waiting for guests. On the right is the library, fitted in Manx bog oak from Lough Malar. Just the place for Poly boys to write their love letters. The drawing-room is on the left, opening by French windows into the lovely grounds. This is no jerry-built affair. The walls are three feet thick as a rule, and two feet and a half is quite thin in other parts. The buildings group around an oblong courtyard, defended by a stout wall. The old moat has disappeared, but a fine macchiolated gateway remains close to the base of the old tower. A secret chamber or two are upstairs. As yet no ghosts are reported, but if any appear their presence will be due to the excellency of Mrs Deas' catering and the indiscretions of a Manx appetite. The Manx tailless cat claims her pedigree from a cat known here in the reign of Elizabeth. The wooded crest of Skyhill stands out against the sunset like a guardian giant at the back of the Park. There, in 1075, was fought the battle of Skoogar Fell. On the ridge is a ruined chapel dating before the Scandinavian invasion. Glen Auldyn, loveliest of Manx valleys, opens at its base. An old-time mill-wheel plashes merrily among the trees in the rear of the house, the water winding down from the gorge above. Oak, ash, elm, and fir jealously unite to guard our paradise on every side. Shady walks, pretty seats, lovely flowers, tennis lawn, shrubberies, and a stone-walled kitchen garden complete our Eden. Our programme includes excursions to Belfast, Douglas, Laxey, Port Erin, Snaefell, Castletown &c. The whole country is rich in historic treasures, and the beauty of hill and dale, wood and fell, gorge and torrent, must be seen to be believed.

Milntown still stands today, a splendid box of Strawberry Gothic white. That Poly tour certainly sounded idyllic, as did so many of the holidays which various authors described to the Polytechnic community. Of course, there is an element of promotion and censorship (or self-censorship) at play here. The Polytechnic and PTA were hardly likely to draw attention to the comments of anyone who did not enjoy holidays with them.

There was rather less unanimity about the purposes and benefits of holidays and foreign travel, as we shall see in a later chapter. However, first we shall examine Polytechnic writers' portrayals of the various types of 'abroad' and how they fitted into the authors' world views. Was there such a thing as a Polytechnic view of the world?

Chapter 7

Meeting Jean le Foreigner:
What the Tourists Thought

In the previous chapter we saw some of the ways in which Polytechnic tourists spent their time on holiday: a mixture of walking expeditions, sightseeing, sport, educational interludes and some fun with a touch of naughtiness. Another aspect of travel though, is to encounter people from elsewhere. While Polytechnic parties did not often give the impression that this was their first priority, they had plenty to say on the subject.

Their views and perceptions could not escape the wider context of the times. In international diplomatic terms, with the Empire at its zenith, the British government was engaged in attempting to maintain its world pre-eminence. Much of this involved defending existing Imperial gains. The revolt of some Transvaal Afrikaners in South Africa and uprising by army officers in Egypt, during 1880–1, posed clear problems to British policymakers in terms of defending vital trade routes to India, Ceylon, Malaya, Burma, Australia and New Zealand. The British occupation of Egypt in 1882 created a direct disagreement with the French, with whom Britain had previously acted jointly in that region.

Britain also kept an anxious eye on its European rivals as they attempted to expand their own empires. As the 'Great Game' continued in Asia, the shadow of Russian involvement fell over the second Afghan War of 1879–82 and, by 1891, Russian forces were rumoured to be massing in the high Pamirs. Under Bismarck, Germany endeavoured to acquire colonies round the world, notably in Africa, and to improve relations with France. The French, meanwhile, had moved into Senegal and annexed Tunisia by 1881, and there were general scares about a possible French invasion of Britain in 1888 and 1900. Out of these years of manoeuvrings and diplomatic crises – including the long drawn out Boer War – came a gradual British diplomatic movement closer to France and Russia, culminating in the Triple Entente after 1907.

Meanwhile, on the frontier between domestic and foreign policy, the Irish Question overshadowed the period. In the late 1880s and early 1890s in particular, it polarised British political party positions, with Conservatives and Liberal Unionists lining up to oppose the Home Rule plans of William Gladstone's Liberal Party, plans which gained support in the House of Commons from the Irish Nationalists. If the Englishman on the Clapham omnibus – or perhaps on the Tube – saw Irish people as somehow different from him, separated by more than just the Irish Sea, perhaps it was not surprising. However, we shall return to Polytechnic thoughts on the Irish later.

Travel seems to have been a part of the Polytechnic's collective DNA from its earliest days – indeed, from the days before Quintin Hogg moved his operations to Regent Street. Hogg was a regular international traveller and wrote home to his charges. His letters, and those of his wife Alice, were sometimes the lead item in *Home Tidings*; they invariably took several pages and, on occasion, as much as half of an entire issue.

Hogg's travel destinations were not always those which Polytechnic parties followed in later years. Nonetheless, many of the comments and assumptions in his travel letters found their echoes in later travel accounts from Polytechnic and PTA tours. Writing in late 1879 about a trip to Pompeii, Hogg's perceptions of the locals are confined to one irritable observation:

I must tell you that each of the principal hotels sends an omnibus and a touter to meet every train, and unless the traveller is prepared to take the law into his own hands, his luggage is carried away forcibly from him by about half-a-dozen different Italian conductors, whose language he can't speak, and whom he sees driving away triumphantly with his boxes on their respective 'buses to various parts of the town, in the hope that the owner will make up his mind to follow and patronise the hotel which they represent.

Naturally, having their own courier, Hogg's party avoided this problem. Most of the rest of the letter describes what they saw at Pompeii and other historical sites. The locals were no more than a passing annoyance.

A month later, the group had reached India. The main point of Hogg's letter this time (published in March 1880) was a lengthy exposition on the Indian Mutiny of 1857. Only as a secondary priority did Hogg describe contemporary

India, although he paused to congratulate himself on spotting an attempt by local dealers to con the 'credulous' into buying fake jewels. He did, however, relate one remarkable encounter with royalty, namely 'a Kokand prince who, having been driven from his kingdom in Central Asia by the Russian Government, has taken refuge on our territory, and is kept in good humour by the magnificent pension of £60 per month allowed him by the Indian Government.' The king himself was

> [A] *desolate-looking youth of about 26, with his hair cut very short, his complexion yellow, and the lozenge shaped tendency of his eyes speaking unmistakeably of his Tartar origin.*
>
> *He came up to us and shook hands in European manner, and gave us to understand, through our interpreter, that he took our visit kindly, and rather liked being "interviewed"…*
>
> [He] *looked harmless enough, and certainly his dress betokened more barbarism than civilisation. He wore a bright blue satin dressing gown ornamented with gorgeous flowers, from beneath which his feet peeped out, clad in some badly-shaped and ill-fitting European boots. His prime minister stood at his side clad in a dressing gown of a much less gorgeous aspect, and apparently exercising his ingenuity in shoving each hand as far as possible up the sleeves of his dress, so as to make the two arms of his dressing gown join together, completely hiding both hands and wrists. The minister, however, had a face of some ability, and he often joined in the conversation, illustrating and enlarging on his master's remarks. After declining an offer of a cup of tea, we said good-bye to our Kokand friend, and expressed our sympathy for his forlorn condition, though we did not tell him that just now there were a good many kings knocking about in search of thrones…*

Clearly Hogg enjoyed the opportunity for a little social climbing, even if he was talking with foreign royalty rather than Queen Victoria herself. His admiration for foreigners diminished, if we are to believe his own accounts, as encounters went down the social scale. As the party left Sri Lanka in the British India Steam Navigation Company's steamship *Africa*, Hogg confessed that he had

> [N]*o great fancy for sailing in foreign vessels, partly because I have a strong aversion to putting money into the pockets of foreigners instead of those of my*

own countrymen, and partly because I should like to be surrounded with English
sailors if matters really came to a crisis at sea.

Years of further travel did not mellow Hogg's views, nor weaken his belief in
the innate superiority of the British and their beneficial effects on the rest of the
world. Here is his view from the Straits of Malacca in 1889:

Quiet and smooth seas are these, but they have been the scene of many a bold
buccaneering deed since the days of good Queen Bess, when French and English
and Dutch alternately saluted each other's flags, and cut each other's throats, till
the commencement of the present century left us with our big National Debt, but
the undisputed hero of the hour, and able to dictate pretty well what terms we
pleased to our neighbours. Then came

THE PAX BRITANNICA
for the East. Malay pirates were hunted down until piracy became an altogether
unprofitable occupation, and now the Malay seems to have relapsed into one
of the mildest and almost indolent races on the face of the earth. There is still,
of course, attached to his name a sufficiently good old bloodthirsty flavour to
enable him to figure splendidly in "Dick Wildrake," or as a chance visitor at the
historical shop of "Sweeny Todd," but as a matter of fact, your genuine Malay
eats and sleeps, but works as little as he can. I believe he does sometimes move
at the time of the rice harvest, but during all other seasons of the year he is
quiescent to an extent utterly puzzling to an Englishman. He can hardly be said
to hibernate for he has no winter, but if he does not look out he will soon find the
Peninsula named after him taken over bodily by the Indian and Chinese coolies,
who are rapidly settling down to do the work which he neglects.

That same year, as we have seen, Robert Mitchell and others were taking a
jaundiced view of their Parisian hosts. Mitchell described the ability of the locals
to extract money from British tourists as resembling a 'spider'. This, along with
JRWK's 'officious individual' two years before, the efforts of Mr St Claire to
overcome 'the natural dislike that the ordinary Parisian entertains for physical
exercise', and the disdain of a party of plumbers for sanitary arrangements at

Rouen, did not add up to a positive overall impression of French people in the early Poly years.

In part this was because Polytechnic parties seem to have had a strong sense of their collective identity. Others were either an admiring audience or got in the way, as ONE WHO WENT made clear in describing an 1888 excursion to Boulogne. Having 'amused ourselves and the passengers' with songs on the outward journey, the party landed at Cape Griznez:

> *Here our trouble, if any, commenced. Being fourteen in number we were beseiged with interpreters and hotel keepers, who asked us all sorts of impossible questions, but, trusting to our own guide, we soon shook these off, only to be pested by boys for* un petit sou.

The adventure resumed after this temporary irritation. Clearly the author and his party felt they could enjoy their day out without 'help' from the locals, or any particular interaction with them for that matter. In a similar vein, JH Freeman had resigned himself to 'a lot of physical discomforts, but they were really reduced to a minimum', when he visited Paris in early 1890. Freeman praised the efforts of Mitchell and his assistant Joseph Bird:

> *[O]ne was inclined to forget the anxiety and trouble he must have had to arrange things so cheaply and well, when every Parisian was expecting, as it were, to coin gold from the visitors, and lighten "John Bull's" purse with some "Exhibition" charges of an exorbitant kind.*

Even ten years later, when the wonderfully-named Mr Bossy met another Polytechnic party for a holiday in Paris and the Bois de Boulogne, the only French to feature in Charles Latham's report were attendants, waiters and stewards at Ecole St Barbe where the group stayed. The 'first-class' holiday experienced no disruption, or apparent input, from other locals.

Not until 1901, and an uncredited account of a holiday in Brittany, do we get any serious attempt by a Polytechnic writer to depict French people as anything other than nuisances or worse. This tour, under the leadership of Louis Graveline, arrived at St Malo on 7 August 1901 and 'commenced operations on French eatables with an energy which astonished the natives (it takes a great deal to astonish a Breton'. From here the party moved on to Dinan, which the author saw in historical terms:

Dinan, with its old thirteenth century castle, from which one can see hills twenty miles away; its Rue de Jersual, dating from the thirteenth century; its old gateways, lighted up at night with candle lanterns; no tramways, no omnibuses, no cabs; everybody taking life as it comes, and looking remarkably healthy; no theatres, no music halls, no Poly Parliament, no hurry; old women spinning by hand outside their cottages… the ramparts specially built as a protection against the English in the Middle Ages…

The writer reprised this general theme when the party moved on to Vannes: 'No hurry, no beggars; everybody with a smile of welcome for strangers; the only ones wearing a dejected look being the Parisian Hussars quartered there.' The piece reads almost as if the writer can cope with French people if they are, in some way, assigned to a historical place, rather than representing a current political rivalry. In this context, France (or Brittany) might represent an escape from modern, busy, polluted, urbanised, industrialised, bureaucratised, complex life to something simpler.

The party could even rope in some children at Carnac, in order to dispense both pity and charity:

[H]*ere also we came across* French children unable to speak French, *their only means of communication being Breton (bad Welsh), but by means of a display of halfpence, we induced them to join with us round a monolith while Mr Styles took a photograph of the group; by another expenditure of (what was to them) the large sum of 10 centimes we induced one to sing us a song in Breton, and as we were leaving they saluted us with one of the sad wild songs peculiar to Brittany and very fascinating.*

Note that even the reference to language places a French dialogue low in the estimation of the writer; Breton being not merely equivalent to Welsh, but to 'bad' Welsh. Even though the French (or Bretons) had at least managed to feature in this account without being demonised as officious, deceitful or lazy, they still

The peasants were good enough here to allow us to inspect some of their houses, and we were delighted at the cleanliness of the interiors. No great comfort or luxury were to be found, but the life of the people must be very hard, and, judging from the healthy condition of the children, it would appear that luxury is not necessary to ensure good health.

To misquote Oscar Wilde, perhaps the only thing worse than being talked about in such patronising terms was not to be talked about at all. But one or two Polytechnic authors were starting to hint at the perception of a world beyond their own comfortable community. Consider these reflections by Rev John Pate in 1903, as a North Cape cruise party reached Tromso:

On landing we found several Lapps waiting for us, they were dwarfs in size with yellow complexions, flat noses and high cheekbones. They were dressed in reindeer skins and were offering for sale rugs, boots and gloves, pipes and spoons, all made from the hide of the reindeer. In the afternoon we crossed the sound and, landing near a factory where whale blubber was being converted into train oil, went through a birch wood and along a mountain side to the LAPP ENCAMPMENT, that we might see the reindeer. They brought about 200 from the hills, and, when they would have bolted on seeing us, lassoed a few of the leaders and dragged them into an enclosure, the rest following like sheep. We entered the little turf huts in which the Lapps live. A skin spread on some twigs served for carpet, table, chairs and bed. As the Lapps looked very dirty, a lady of our party enquired of a woman how often she washed. "Once in every moon." In answer to a question about her child, the woman replied: "Baby does not need washing; the dogs are fond of him and lick him with their tongues." As one of the Lapps pretended to know English our humorous friend asked "Do you use Pears soap?" "Yah!" "Will you give a testimonial 'I used your soap many years ago, since when I have used no other'?" "Yah!" But if we amused ourselves at their expense they certainly enjoyed our visit and had a quiet laugh as they said "The English are wild geese, they come only in the summer, we pluck them and they fly away."

Finally a local inhabitant on a Polytechnic tour was more than just a cipher or a walking stereotype. There was even the hint that the writer and his party did not have a monopoly on wit.

Another writer, Sheena Macdonald, took this even further in November 1905 with an account of a 'pioneer' Polytechnic tour of Hungary. In this article, Hungarians not only existed, but they had names:

The untiring and invaluable assistance rendered by M. Golonya, who never left the party till its arrival in Budapest, has earned the sincerest thanks of the Poly, Mr Shrubsole [presumably the tour leader] *and all the party; being master of our language as well as his own, his services were always in demand. Nor must we forget here, M. Zoltan Szarvasy, Dr Dezso Nagy, and M. Bela Szlatenyi, the Director of the 'Strangers Ticket Office', who by their presence and help added to the enjoyment and comfort of the tour.*

Plainly there is an element of namedropping here, with the writer demonstrating how well-connected the Polytechnic was in a country which very few of its students and members would have visited. Nonetheless, this was still something quite new in Polytechnic travel reports. Local people were present throughout the report: the Slovaks of the Tatras who 'are said to be very poor and lazy' (a view contradicted by the writer's observation of 'some fine specimens of healthy manhood and women') and a Hungarian poet who 'has said that we cannot put our feelings into words, and this even in his own beautifully expressive language'. Trips to vineyards, wine cellars and a champagne factory might have sat oddly with the beliefs of the more orthodox Polytechnic adherents to temperance. The article concluded:

The trip to Hungary must long linger in our hearts as one of our pleasantest remembrances. May we make it thus for our Hungarian friends when they visit our shores!

Space forbids me writing more about the Hungarian people. One cannot sing their praises too strongly, of their unequalled hospitality and of their sweetly expressive language which lends itself so well to the romance of their nature and surroundings, of the quaintly artistic dresses of the peasantry so truly eastern, giving vivid colouring to the whole scene, and of the characteristic music which alternately makes one weep and sing. These and other traits of interest in the Hungarian life and character may be our theme at some future time. And now we would cry "God bless Hungary and her noble people and bring them safely through their present political crisis without a stain on their fair fame."

The romanticised, but entirely positive, view of the local people, and interest in their culture, was practically unique among Polytechnic tour accounts, as was the implication that the tourists would, some day, return the hospitality they had received.

The writers of Polytechnic travel accounts also had their own views about Ireland and the Irish. The earliest Polytechnic account of a trip to Killamey, and to the nearby Dunloe Castle, dates back to 1890. If the thoughts of the uncredited author are a reliable guide, then the party found the encounter with locals more than a little unsettling:

[A]s we approach Killarney, the sight of the undulating beauties of the country kindles that admiration with which we came prepared, and yet at the same time we cannot help feeling that much of our excitement is due to the striking contrast between the richness and variety of the scenery, and the wretched, open poverty of the people; such poverty it is almost an insult to call picturesque. One thing I must warn trippers against, and that is the exorbitant charges on the journey for anything in the way of food and drink; charges, that if hunger compels you to put up with them, will almost convince you that you are living on a thousand a year, with nothing to do but spend it. It was with feelings of thankfulness that we arrived at Killarney about four o'clock, and found a messenger from Dunloe awaiting us with the jaunting cars. The responsibility of the journey, which had hitherto rested with ourselves, was shifted, and we began at once to be "quite Irish, you know," although it seemed to us that we should never quite be able to comprehend the resolute, sharp-cut brogue of the Kerry men.

Clearly the writer knew that such thoughts about the Irish could be seen as patronising – but could not help expressing them anyway. The following day, a Sunday, gave the party a chance to observe the local people in another context:

In the morning, one party went to the Protestant church with Mr Bird, while another party, under the care of our guide Dan Moriarty (a gamekeeper of the

Lucerne – Polytechnic Chalets

POST CARD

PRINTED MATTER

Miss D. B. Shopee.
"the Hollies"
83. Hosfora Rd.
golden green.
London
N.W.11.

England.

Dear B.

We hope to go here on thursday. Hope I shall not fall over! Have taken no end on snaps already, but feel rather dubious abt. the results. The scenery & colouring here is marvellous. You would never believe it unless you could see it.

POLYTECHNIC SERIES.
PUBLISHED BY THE PHOTOCHROM CO LTD LONDON AND TUNBRIDGE WELLS.

Lucerne Postkarte.

Mr. John Sala
Market Street
Winterton
Via Abercrombie
England

Wehrli A.-G., Kilchberg-Zürich.

Lucérne – Seeburg
Dining – room
Social – room

Weather fine.
Excursion up Pilates
to-day by railway.
Gradient 1 in 2.
Length 3 miles, 7000 ft.
up to the end.
APR.
1902 Le délabranets
...
Beaumont,
Jersey.

Carte Postale

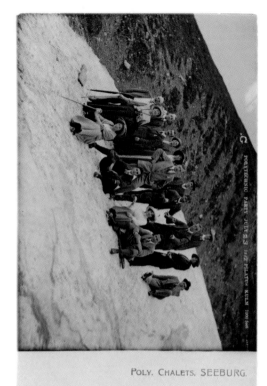

POLY. CHALETS, SEEBURG.

"Hotel Schreiber" Rigi Kulm
Dear Agg. Here we are at the most
picturesque country in the world.
We are playing at the Chalet on
Lake Lucerne. Have come up here for
the day by steamer & wonderful ride
as we rise. Uncle can see the Austrian
Tyrol, Black forest of Germany, Swiss Oberland
Italian Alps & French Alps. just inside
a precipice of 4000 ft. scenery just
glorious. Love from both. Marion

Mrs Mulchinock
"Oxford"
Rumphries Cres
East Malvern
Melbourne
Victoria,
Australia

1714 Seeburg - Lucerne - Polytechnic, Chalets et Stansenhorn

Polytechnic Chalets, Seeburg, Lucerne.

POLYTECHNIC CHALETS

Interlaken, Polytechnic Chalet

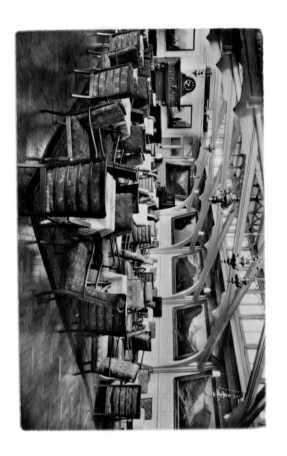

DRUCKSACHE.

PRINTED MATTER.

IMPRIMÉ.

POST CARD

PC

THIS SPACE FOR COMMUNICATION

ADDRESS ONLY

PRINTED IN ENGLAND.

Polytechnic Chalets
Lucerne
Switzerland.

We are having the most
delightful holiday of our lives
in this beautiful place. The
mountains look just lovely,
and everything is done to make
us thoroughly happy & comfortable.
If you have not yet fixed
your holiday send at once for
full particulars of their tours
to The Polytechnic,
309 Regent Street,
London. W.

THE PHOTOCHROM CO., LTD., LONDON & DETROIT U.S.A.
CELESQUE SERIES

W. Thornton Esq
142 Armoley Rd
Leeds
England

THE OLD BRIDGE, LUCERNE.

OLAF. THE DOG WATCH.

POLYTECHNIC NORWAY CRUISES.

THE ROMSDAL

POLYTECHNIC NORWAY CRUISES

"POLY" CRUISES THE SHORE PARTY

S.V. CEYLON.

POLYTECHNIC NORWAY CRUISES

EN ROUTE TO THE LOTEFOSS.   POLYTECHNIC NORWAY CRUISES.

NÆROFJORD.   POLYTECHNIC NORWAY CRUISES.

GEIRANGER FJORD.   POLYTECHNIC NORWAY CRUISES.

FANTOFT CHURCH.   POLYTECHNIC NORWAY CRUISES.

ROMSDAL HORN.

POLYTECHNIC NORWAY CRUISES.

HORNELEN.

POLYTECHNIC NORWAY CRUISES.

MAIN STREET, TRONDHJEM.

POLYTECHNIC NORWAY CRUISES.

S.V. CEYLON.

POLYTECHNIC NORWAY CRUISES.

THE LERFOSS-TRONDHJEM.   POLYTECHNIC NORWAY CRUISES.

Mauranger Fjord

THE BONDHUS GLACIER.   POLYTECHNIC NORWAY CRUISES.

TRONDHJEM CATHEDRAL.   POLYTECHNIC NORWAY CRUISES.

THE NÆRODAL.   POLYTECHNIC NORWAY CRUISES.

BERGEN, FISHMARKET.

POLYTECHNIC NORWAY CRUISES.

ODDE HARDANGER FJORD.

POLYTECHNIC NORWAY CRUISES.

MEROK.

POLYTECHNIC NORWAY CRUISES.

MOLDE.

POLYTECHNIC NORWAY CRUISES.

THE LOTEFOSS.

POLYTECHNIC NORWAY CRUISES.

VOSSEVANGEN.

POLYTECHNIC NORWAY CRUISES.

MEROK.

POLYTECHNIC NORWAY CRUISES.

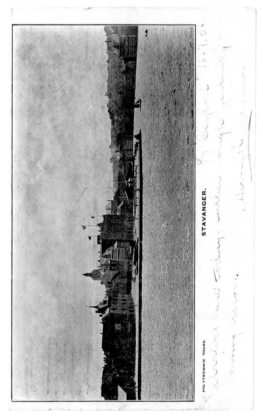

STAVANGER.

POLYTECHNIC TOURS.

MAIN STREET TROMSO.

POLYTECHNIC NORWAY CRUISES.

Most enjoyable.

S.Y. VIKING. THE DINNER CALL.

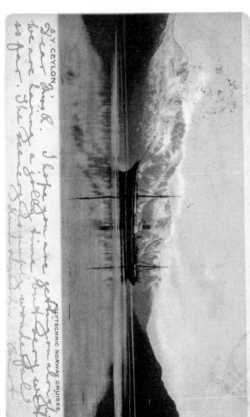

S.Y. CEYLON.

POLYTECHNIC NORWAY CRUISES.

BERGEN THE TORVET.

Having enjoyable Cruise. Jimmy Bradford.

POLYTECHNIC NORWAY CRUISES.

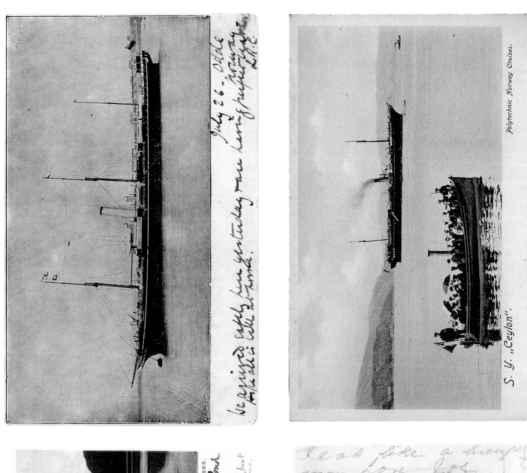

Some hotels which the PTA used are still standing today including including Milntown on the Isle of Man; the chalets at Lucerne (top and bottom left); and the Highland Hotel, Fort William, Scotland.

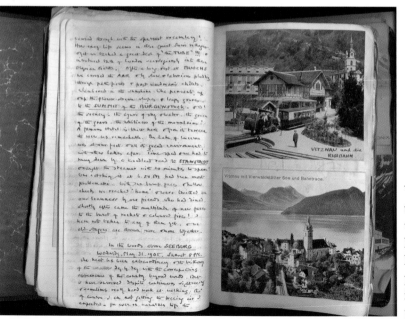

Wilfred Bryant travelled to Switzerland twice with the PTA. Shown here is an extract from his diary along with postcards that he pasted into it as a record of his travels

All of the images are courtesy of the University of Westminster Archives apart from the photos of Lucerne Chalets (Anna McNally) and of Milntown and the Highland Hotel (the author).

*Macgillycuddy's who has already become quite a favourite with us), proceeded
to the Roman Catholic chapel, in order to get some idea of how the "rale native"
kept Sunday. To a stranger, looking at the intense and absorbed worship of the
peasantry, the celebration of mass in a country place in Ireland has a peculiar
attraction that seems to chain one in the power of some mysterious influence. Our
party, made aware of the extreme sensitiveness of the Irish people, behaved in a
way that gained for us the respectful tolerance of the whole congregation, and I
did not see one resentful look at our intrusion.*

Once again, despite the portrayal of clear divisions between the Protestant urban
English tourists and the Catholic rural Irish locals, the outcome was, in the
writer's view, a Polytechnic triumph.

A letter from 'WW' in the 29 May issue of the *Polytechnic Magazine* gave
another glimpse into Polytechnic interactions with the people of Killarney and
the Gap of Dunloe. One aspect of this was to meet a young woman posing as Kate
Kearney, a well-known Irish beauty from the years before the Famine. Legend
had it that Kate offered all weary travellers her 'Mountain Dew', a potent and
illicit local brew. WW and the others met both the 1890 incarnation of Kate
Kearney and other local women:

*Kate Kearney came out of her cottage, and acted as Honorary Rearguard to
the party for about a mile, tempting us with potheen or mountain dew. There
are several weird echoes in the Gap, awakened wither by the Kerry bugle (Dan
is au fait at this), or by small cannon, fired by the natives. At the Head of the
Gap, leaving the rocks behind us, we come suddenly upon a most magnificent
panorama; to our left, and almost under us, lies the upper part of the Killarney
lakes, while on the right is the Black Valley, with a white cataract at the extreme
end. In this hollow we met the prettiest "colleens" it was our privilege to see while
in Ireland. Naturally, they "blarneyed" us a good deal, coaxing and persuading
us to have a drop of the "mountain dew". In several cases their wiles could not
be withstood, so "bang went saxpence". Their home-spun and home-knitted socks
we can highly recommend, and the "colleens" should be encouraged this way a
little, as they informed us they were making up the marriage money, and hoped
before long to be leaving for America.*

In an echo of the previous writer's allusion to the 'sensitivity' of the Irish, WW advised those who might go on future tours of the area: 'Beware of falling into political discussions or arguments on religious subjects, with the natives.'

It is fair to ask whether any of this was unusual, or just the typical set of views and attitudes of the times, which you could find in other reports of English people's holidays in the UK and abroad. In fact, there are notable differences between Polytechnic travel accounts and those that appear in the inhouse journals for other emerging travel agencies such as Toynbee Hall and the CHA.

Partly the differences reflect a wider difference in locations visited. Most travel reports and logbooks for the Toynbee Travellers' Club and its offshoot Workmen's Travelling Club focused on Italy, France and Belgium, while CHA articles were devoted primarily to holidays in England but also in Germany and France. The CHA holidays were normally to rural locations, seeking 'a glorious outdoor existence' of walks, clean air and clear streams. Toynbee tours had more explicitly academic and cultural aims; a 1903 trip to Germany visited an opera house, something which rarely featured on Polytechnic itineraries. Neither Toynbee nor the CHA visited Switzerland nearly so often, with anything like as many tourists, as the Polytechnic did.

Partly the difference was also a matter of gender. Unlike the Polytechnic which, after all, started life as a club for young men, female authors were a regular presence in *Comradeship* (the CHA journal) and the *Toynbee Herald*. As travel writing by female authors was by no means unusual at this time, the Polytechnic accounts were the 'odd man out' in this respect.

But, on top of these variations, Toynbee and CHA travel accounts simply didn't report their authors' travels in the same way as the Polytechnic. The emphasis on the impression that the touring party made on the locals – not to mention the namedropping of encounters with eminent persons up to and including princes and emperors – wasn't there. A Toynbee travel writer would remark on how the local populace 'came to stare', and a CHA author might become the object of foreign curiosity, such as R Thomson who recalled how two retired German ladies wanted to know what the CHA was.

The superiority which Polytechnic writers always implied for themselves – and by implication England or Britain – over the inhabitants of France, in particular, was not so manifest in Toynbee or CHA writings. CHA authors observed with approval, for example, that a lesser degree of income inequality existed in Germany than in Britain and that Continental people had more opportunities for holidays than the British. Toynbee articles and logbooks described 'scenes [from] popular life' such as the drawing of the municipal lottery in Bologna, and had kind words for the Italians, the Germans and the Dutch, among others. The CHA's internationalist outlook, meanwhile, set it aside from Polytechnic parties' relative indifference towards the indigenous populations of the places they visited. TA Leonard described the purpose of a fortnight in Germany as being 'the creation of friendly feelings between the two countries'. 'FBS' described similarities and differences between Germans and Britons, concluding that 'the dividing things are in their nature superficial [whereas] the matters of union are fundamental'. CHA travel authors also recognised and welcomed Britain's new diplomatic closeness with France.

Relatively little evidence survives of what foreigners, and for that matter other British people, thought of the Polytechnic and PTA holidaymakers. The Rev Canon John William Horsley was moved to comment in these terms upon encountering a group in Meiringen, Switzerland, in 1892:

> One evening there trudged into the hotel garden a part of unmistakable London lads, clerks and shopmen mainly, weary somewhat with the long walk from the Furka Pass. They were from the Regent Street Polytechnic, and when I found that a fortnight in Switzerland had cost under eight pounds, I first marvelled at what co-operation and contrivance and contracts could effect; then, turning my thoughts to grimy Woolwich, I began to wonder whether 'Woolwich in the Alps' was an impossibility.

Whether this view revealed a greater degree of admiration or condescension is debatable. Others were less ambivalent, particularly if the Poly parties enjoyed themselves. The 16 September 1902 edition of the *Berwickshire News and General Advertiser* noted:

> The Polytechnic Touring Coy., London, sent 120 tourists here on Thursday. They visited Thirlestane Castle and the Parish Church, after which they put up

at the Black Bull Hotel, and had lunch which Mr Sheppard had prepared for them in his usual excellent way. The visitors then departed in coaches (which Mr Wilson had in readiness) for Melrose, Abbotsford, and Dryburgh, then to St Boswells, where a special train was waiting to convey them to Edinburgh. They were all delighted with their lovely drive, especially through Lauderdale and the Land of Scott.

The *Isle of Man Times* (12th September 1903) reported on the visit of a party of 130 Polytechnic tourists on the *SS Ceylon*, cruising round Britain and stopping for a while on the island, at Douglas and Ramsey. The Speaker of the House of Keys and 'other prominent citizens' of Douglas visited the *Ceylon* and the tourists regretfully declined an invitation to the Palace Theatre.

Without doubt, the Polytechnic travel accounts as a whole did convey a 'Polytechnic view' in a distinctive 'Polytechnic voice'. Whether recounting the experiences of bonding with each other on the outward journey, attending Sunday services on land and at sea, causing consternation among the natives, playing their favourite sports or portraying themselves as representatives of the Polytechnic, Britain and the Empire. The travel accounts created a vivid picture of a Polytechnic 'bubble' within which members, students and others could enjoy their holidays. Written and published at a time when the British Empire was at its zenith, albeit coming under increasingly intensive challenges from various quarters, these travel accounts did not allow much room for doubt: of the writer, of the Polytechnic or of the wider imperial context.

Perhaps most fascinatingly, while the Polytechnic tours owed their creation to a large degree to 'rational recreation' and their presumed educational/ improving benefits were promoted, like those of Toynbee Hall and the CHA, the travel accounts indicate that Polytechnic holidays were more than the sum of their origins. Polytechnic tourists might well attend church services abroad, for example, at sea – where they could presumably scarcely be avoided – or early in the holiday before getting down to the 'real business', which could involve visiting mines and factories, but would mostly consist of seeing sights and relaxing in good company. Some of the capers reported in *Home Tidings* and the *Polytechnic Magazine* had a distinct whiff of slapstick and the music hall about them. CHA and Toynbee travellers might well have believed they, too, were having fun, but they did not write about it to anything like the same extent. We can acknowledge that definitions of fun and enjoyment did, and do, differ, while still recognising something distinctive about the Polytechnic accounts.

Chapter 8

The Purpose of Holidays: A Modern Note?

In previous chapters we saw where Polytechnic touring parties went on holidays. Mostly these were to continental Europe – Switzerland and Norway being especially popular – and within the British Isles to a host of destinations including Scotland and Ireland. Some aspects of the tours had overt educational overtones, but there was plenty of time for climbing mountains, walking across glaciers, fishing and playing sport, dashing round cities' sights and bonding as a group, on steamboats, in church or by the piano in the evenings. We have also seen that those who reported on the tours, including some Polytechnic officials who led them, did not place a high priority on meeting foreigners (or 'internal' foreigners such as Scottish and Irish locals). It took over a decade of travel accounts in the *Polytechnic Magazine* for the writers to suppress, or even lessen, a general attitude of superiority and, in the case of the French, distaste for their perceived attempts to con honest Englishmen out of their money. The pleasures of a mostly self-contained Polytechnic 'bubble' outweighed the potential pleasures of interacting with the natives.

But if the purpose of going on holiday wasn't to meet Johnny Foreigner, what was it? The answer varied, depending on who was giving it. While there may have been an 'official' view, as expressed by Quintin Hogg, in Polytechnic publications or at events, this did not mean that the holidaymakers accepted that line – and disagreements could be vehement.

An obvious place at which to reflect on their holidays was a reunion, or 'social' as some Polytechnic authors who reported the events for the magazine called them. The reunions were normally organised by holiday location. The first to be reported was a 'social' in October 1889 for members of the Young Women's Institute who had attended the Paris Exhibition. An equivalent event for members of the Young Men's Institute who had been to Paris took place the following February. The numbers attending varied from around 200 for a Rhine Tour reunion to an estimated 5,000 for a Swiss Tours event. Larger events had to be held in the Queen's Hall to accommodate the attendees. As a mark of the national reach of the Polytechnic tours, reunions sometimes took place in provincial centres such as Manchester and Bristol. Some remarks upon a Norway reunion from September 1891 convey an impression of the atmosphere:

> *The arrangements were carried out on the most elaborate scale. The Large Hall being found inadequate, the Gymnasium and old Reading Room were specially requisitioned for the occasion. The old Reading Room made an admirable reception room, where the genial stewards received their guests and escorted them to the floor of the Gymnasium, where the tea tables were invitingly displayed. Some 500 sat down to tea, the Orchestral Band dispensed sweet music during this preliminary "ceremony." Each party of excursionists were accommodated at separate tables, and many were the hand-shakings and greetings after the long separation of—some few weeks. The room itself presented a lively appearance, the fearful machinery upon which the daring gymnast disports his manly form being carefully stowed away, and what remained of his implements of warfare were tastefully covered with inoffensive bunting and rampant flags alive with the crests of all Europe.*
>
> *After tea the assembly transferred itself to the Large Hall ... The ex-excursionists settled down in their new quarters, and spent some thirty minutes' interval in comparing notes of the vicissitudes and hardships incurred during their sojourn in foreign lands under the auspices of the Poly flag. Mr Hogg's appearance was the signal to commence the more serious business of the evening...*

Though the sequence of events varied, reunions generally consisted of a welcome with tea and refreshments; speeches; reconstructions of the holidays using photographs, magic lantern slides and cinematographs; presentations of gifts to tour leaders; and musical performances, recitals and other diversions, often closing with 'Auld Lang Syne' or the National Anthem. Guests sometimes got more than they bargained for. During tea at one reunion in 1895, 'Mr Harding caused much amusement by administering shocks to the ladies with his electric battery.' Hogg occasionally chaired the reunions, but this duty, especially for larger events, fell more frequently to Mitchell or, in the case of reunions of Scottish trips, Studd.

Reunions added several stages to the process of promoting tours. In addition to reading the publicity for a tour, going on that tour and reading a report of the tour, Polytechnic members and students could also obtain advance information on the reunion event; attend that reunion, several months after the tour; and finally read about it in the *Polytechnic Magazine*. In this way, reunions helped the Polytechnic to maintain awareness of its tours for the best part of a calendar year.

Although, as we have seen, the earliest tours had educational origins, tour reunions (or at least the reports of them in the *Polytechnic Magazine*) did not tend to focus on the educational benefits of travel. If anything, as the tours became an established and popular part of Polytechnic life, there was a temptation to underplay this angle. 'WGL', the author of several reunion reports, made a cheekily subversive reference in 1900 to the ground-breaking 1888 Swiss trip, praising a presentation by Mitchell as 'not a geography lesson, but a most entertaining holiday yarn'. In a 1905 report, WGL commented, more respectfully, that:

> *As a means of education, such a visit is unparalleled. The only text book required is a prospectus of the tours, and the acceptance of its invitation secures an entrance to a valuable course of study in geography, history and economics.*

Other reunion reports gave various suggestions as to the ways in which travel could benefit the tourist. An 1891 writer used the metaphor of slot machines to suggest that holidays reinvigorated those who went on them: 'In future … you will put not your penny but yourself into the slot, and, well, there you are, you will come back with your machinery wound up to go for twelve months, guaranteed.' Others laid emphasis on the sociability and good fellowship of the reunions and, by extension, the tours themselves. During one rendition of 'Auld Lang Syne', the audience 'shook hands all round till their arms ached in sympathy with their sorely-tried sides'. Another report reflected that 'the invariable success of these reunions shows how heartily our friends enjoy such opportunities of meeting again to ramble over the holiday haunts and renew the acquaintances made in such pleasant circumstances in the summer.' The chalet arrangements at Lucerne enabled tourists to feel they were 'more like a great family'. Reports of reunions in 1910 and 1911 praised the opportunities to enjoy 'the speech of a trusty friend, the singing of a good song, and the recital of a happy yarn' and claimed that the 'secret reason for the success of the tours arranged by the Polytechnic [were the i]nexhaustible ... resources of the country [Switzerland] to give pleasure, and with pleasure health.'

Hogg's thoughts on the purposes and benefits of holidays did not generally find their way into reunion reports, except on the occasion of the aforementioned September 1891 Norway reunion. Hogg rose and:

> [I]n a few happy sentences, [he] voiced the sentiments of all present in describing these trips as more than mere holiday jaunts, emphasising the power for good such travels may become - above all, the bringing the created into direct sympathy with the Creator.

Others also gave occasional hints of more serious motivations. Councillor Hughes, a Bristol dignitary who hosted a Polytechnic reunion in the city in 1897, approved of the temperance principles on which the tours ran. The councillor believed that 'trips on the Continent did a great deal to ensure peace between nations. It used to be only the nobility who could enjoy the pleasure of travel, but now it was open to all.'

The question of how accessible Polytechnic holidays truly were became, and remained, a matter of contention for some of its members. Doubts about the accessibility of Polytechnic holidays to its least affluent members and students on the grounds of cost, and sometimes on the basis of their timing during the year, had surfaced as early as 1890. That summer's holiday homes included a camp in Deal, courtesy of the London Diocesan Council for Welfare of Young Men, for the use of Polytechnic members for 5s for a fortnight. The editorial announcing this initiative admitted that some Polytechnic holidays were too dear for 'many of our younger members'. In the following week's letters column, 'ABH' suggested that 'a large proportion of members who have to take their holidays in August' could not, therefore go to Ireland or Switzerland, and suggested a fortnight's excursion in mid-August to North Wales or any one of 'scores of places in the British Isles'. ABH did, however, add that members could organise such a trip themselves if the Polytechnic authorities did not.

Council meetings became a forum in which members raised concerns about the tours. The 1891 Norway tours, it was feared, might end up catering for more 'outsiders' than members – a worry that informed planning the use of the Jersey home two years later, when non-member bookings were barred until after 23rd May. A Council meeting of 9 February 1892, attended by representatives of the governing body, heard a discussion about 'the more expensive foreign trips, some of the members of the council bringing forward arguments against them which they had heard urged amongst their friends away from the Institute.' The arguments were: that 'comparatively few' members could afford the £25–30 needed for a foreign holiday, or could obtain the time; that it was 'improper' to use Institute funds for such tours; that those who could afford such holidays could obtain them through other routes and were of 'quite a different social position to that for which the Institute was intended'; that there should be more UK seaside holiday homes instead; and that more places should be reserved for members, with 'their option [being] extended to a later date'.

Hogg responded that (in relation specifically to the planned 1893 Chicago trip) those who could afford it would gain great educational value and that 'the trip must not be looked upon from a holiday point of view only'; that the trips did not use Institute funds, but made a profit and promoted the Polytechnic's work in the provinces; that aiding those outside the Polytechnic's 'intended' sphere would 'materially assist … in various ways'; that the expenses of foreign trips did not affect the establishment of other UK holiday homes; and that no member to his knowledge who had applied to go on a Norway trip had missed out.

Clearly this subject rankled with some Council members, as another lengthy discussion followed a few weeks later, with a sub-committee formed to discuss suggestions for expanding the UK holiday homes and tours arrangements. However, the specific proposals of North and South Devon, North Wales and Scarborough as locations for 'about a fortnight's holiday at a cost of from £5 to £6' did not make it into the Polytechnic's touring programme for that year. North Wales and Scarborough did not appear in the Polytechnic portfolio till 1895 and 1904 respectively. As late as 1899, another Council sub-committee was overseeing holiday homes in Eastbourne, Hastings and Margate for between 26s and 27s 6d per week. 'As there are members who are not able to afford so much as this,' the sub-committee also announced the taking of a home at Westgate-on-Sea (near Margate) for a week in July and three weeks in August – in connection with the Holiday by Proxy Fund:

[T]o reserve this house entirely for members whose means are too limited to pay the full cost of a holiday ... Should there be any who through sickness or other misfortunes are not even able to pay the reduced fees, the committee will be glad to consider any such application, and arrangements will be made to provide a free holiday in connection with the Holiday-by-Proxy Fund. The authorities hope that, as a result of these arrangements, none of our members will have to forgo a seaside holiday.

It is not clear whether any members made such applications or, if they did so, how the Polytechnic responded. Nonetheless, it is a striking sign of the concern of the Polytechnic authorities that any members should be unable to afford a cheap seaside holiday. The Holiday by Proxy Fund was originally set up as a philanthropic initiative for the benefit of poor families living near the Polytechnic; here it was being used (or made available for use) for philanthropy aimed at the Polytechnic's own members.

The interaction of the mainstream holiday home portfolio and the Holiday by Proxy Fund was the focus of dissension and debate in one other case. In July 1894 the Polytechnic announced the securing of Lewisham House, Weston-super-Mare, claiming it had done so on the basis of requests from members 'by way of a change from ... Clacton and Ramsgate'. The new home would be available between August and mid-September for 33s 6d per week. The following year, the Holiday by Proxy Fund secured a house for nominated people - at Clacton. The first party of sixteen arrived at the house on 6th July 1895.

With Clacton's replacement by Weston-super-Mare as a mainstream holiday home for members, the letters column of the *Polytechnic Magazine* began to resemble a multi-player tennis match, with various members lamenting the change – and suggesting that the Polytechnic was neglecting its own – and Hogg or the *Polytechnic Magazine* editor, Samson Clark, defending it.

'FGH' opened the debate in the *Magazine*'s 12 June edition:

On looking through the excellent list of holiday arrangements for 1895, one cannot help observing the very meagre attention which is paid to holidays in Great Britain for fellows with a modest purse at their disposal. While rejoicing to see the Poly taking the lead in organising trips to all parts of Europe, it appears to me that the fellows for whom our Institute was founded are to a certain extent neglected. For the member desirous of a fortnight's holiday at a cost of between £4 and £5 (of whom there are many in the Poly.), there are only two possible trips advertised, viz. Weston and the Ardennes. The latter is doubtless very enjoyable, but many prefer exploring the beauties of Great Britain to rushing abroad, and spending the only fortnight of the year in a more tiring fashion. Only Weston, therefore, is eligible to the member who requires a holiday which recruits his health, and permits him to see some good scenery. Under the able management of Mr and Mrs Deas the Weston Home is a very enjoyable one, but only available for some six weeks, so that to him whose holiday does not fall within that time, or would like to go rather farther away, there is nothing whatever offered. Consequently every year a great number of our members are thrown upon their own resources, instead of being catered for by the Institute, whereas to the outsider who can spend more heavily, every facility is given in many trips from June to October. Surely it is not too much to ask that a little of that splendid organising ability which the officials possess should be devoted to the needs of the Poly boy. Cannot the Killarney trips be restarted for this season? Or a tour through Devon and Cornwall? I feel confident there are many who will agree with me on this question.

Hogg explained in reply that the 'exceptional terms' the Polytechnic could obtain for its members depended on sufficient numbers booking the tours and that Killarney 'left a loss'. However, this did not mollify Robert Dredge, whose letter appeared the following week:

The letter signed "F.G.H." in the last issue of the MAG is quite true regarding the holiday list being confined to the outside public, whereas the Poly boys are given only Weston or nothing. At a meeting of Poly fellows (which I arranged) held last Friday, it was decided by those present to ask the Poly officials to extend the list so as to include (say) North Wales or Isle of Man. I have seen Mr Studd about it, but he says it is a mistaken idea of mine, for the majority of the Institute would prefer Weston. I am sure Mr Studd is mistaken, not I. Hoping the Poly officials will take steps at once and arrange for (the ungracious?) faithfully yours…

Even for an institution used to debate and disagreement, this was strong stuff. In reply, Samson Clark sarcastically remarked that 'the writers seems to have overlooked' the arrangements at Hastings, Eastbourne and Brighton 'as well as the Ardennes trip, which is surely within the reach of a large number of our members.'

That seemed to be that... until four weeks later when the letters column returned to the subject, this time with a message from WH Jones:

In a club notice on 3rd inst. the Holiday-by-Proxy Fund announced that they had taken a house at Clacton and had sent down a staff to manage it. If a small band of workers dependent upon subscriptions can do this how is it that the Institute Committee cannot take a house at Clacton instead of Weston? Anyone who has visited both places will, I am sure, agree with me that Clacton is by far the most beneficial for fellows who, say for fifty-one weeks in a year, are penned up in a hot workshop or office. Weston is all very well for the class of people the Institute are now arranging trips for viz., the "well-to-do," but it is not the place for anyone who has to work hard for a living to go to recruit their health. I was at Weston last year, and the sea(!) during my week resembled the river Thames more than anything else, both as regards mud at low water and the colour of the water when the tide was up. Yours truly, WH JONES [who gave his membership number as 24,578]

Samson Clark's response was not sympathetic: 'No. 24,578 is behind the times' as the Poly had abandoned its previous Clacton base at the wish of members. Clark added that 'Clacton ... has no recommendations either of beauty, excursions, or historical interest. The only endurable thing about it is its fresh air, and one's enjoyment of that is largely marred by its obtrusively cockney excursionists.'

The following week, 24 July, Charles Cronin supported Jones' views and disputed Samson Clark's description of Clacton:

I may say that the "fresh air" is not the only endurable thing about Clacton; such good-fellowship as was my great delight to experience at both Clacton and Ramsgate I have never before or since come in contact with on a holiday, and I, as well as others, showed our appreciation of its benefits, and our regret at its abandonment, so plainly that we almost got ourselves disliked for so doing.

He asked: 'How many Institute members, earning 25s. a week, can afford to spend £4 8s for a week's holiday? Those with small earnings are entirely left out in the cold.' The Editor replied that cheaper alternatives were available and that 'As to Clacton and its visitors, we must agree to differ.'

Clearly Samson Clark did not wish the Polytechnic to associate itself with 'cockneys' (at least, not on holidays). Gareth Stedman Jones has argued that sympathetic mid-century representations of the 'cockney' had given way by this time to caricatures (for example, of ''Arry' in *Punch*) which highlighted his loud, vulgar qualities. He was the sort to enjoy loud singsongs in third class railway carriages, to become rowdy in his natural social habitats of music hall and pub. Stedman Jones describes a typical candidate for 'cockney' status as being a clerk who might earn £2 a week and be entitled to two weeks of annual holidays. If we accept this as a plausibly accurate depiction of the 1890s 'cockney', no wonder one or two Polytechnic members reacted sharply to Clark's comments; they might have felt that his description was a little too close to home. This exchange between a key manager and other members of a London-based institution placed the Polytechnic, and its members, on the fault lines of the continuing tensions between respectable lower middle class 'travellers' and cockney 'tourists'.

The Clacton issue rumbled on into the new century, with *Magazine* correspondents continuing to criticise the cost of holiday homes and foreign tours as being beyond the reach of some members. There was also grumbling about the use of commercial guesthouses rather than 'the old Poly Holiday Home … [which] was much more suitable in every way than the alternative now offered of a week's holiday with strangers, when the very existence of the Poly YMCI [Young Men's Christian Institute] is lost sight of.'

Nor could the tours escape occasional criticism as part of a wider discourse regarding the balance of activities and purposes within the Polytechnic. Charles Pratt, the honorary secretary of the Polytechnic Harriers and a member of the Polytechnic Men's Council, used the Harriers column of the *Polytechnic Magazine* to state:

> I am at one with those who consider the sociability of our Institute is being extremely neglected. If one grumbles we are asked for a remedy. This is easily found, only the trouble is to get those in authority to see it. The cause is this. Energies that would be engrossed in helping along the social side of the Institute,

and in the old days did so, are now entirely taken up with the promotion of "globetrotting" expeditions, by which outsiders are mainly (in fact, solely) benefited. No doubt this sort of thing is very meritorious, and the running of a trip a guinea cheaper than Cook's is beneficial to well-to-do men (who could easily pay the difference). When, however, this is done at the expense of our Institute, then I for one say, reasonably curtail your programme, and come back to Institute work. Many hundreds of Poly fellows are of my way of thinking …

In a follow-up letter, Pratt wrote that trips 'should be curtailed or, at any rate, not be allowed to take up the whole of the energies of those who are best adapted to assist in the genuine Institute work' if they interfered with 'sociability' within the Polytechnic. In reply, Hogg characterised criticism by Pratt and others as falling into three categories: that Polytechnic work was being 'sacrificed' to foreign trips too expensive for the average 'Poly boy'; that education was taking undue priority over other matters; and that the social side of the Polytechnic was being neglected. With regard to the first point, he stated that:

I doubt if there ever was in the Institute more sociability than at present, but, with our increasing numbers, it naturally concentrates itself more and more in sections … As for myself I have been four days a week at the Poly, all through the autumn, the other three days having been spent at one or other of the Poly Homes. Indeed, if you except my business absence last Christmas, and two short absences with Poly trips to Rome and Lucerne respectively, I have not been seven consecutive days away from the Institute for five and a half years. I say, then, that I do not think there is any foundation for the assertion that our social life has been neglected for the trips, while the trips themselves have been, not only an effective advertisement, but a source of revenue … It is far from our wish to turn the Poly, into a mere academy, and no one impartially regarding it could say that this has been done.

In all likelihood, with such a large membership and an increasingly diverse range of activities, it would have been impossible for the Polytechnic to devise a programme of British and overseas holidays which could be completely accessible, affordable and acceptable to all its members (not to mention students and non-members). The numbers of Polytechnic holidaymakers continued to rise. Even so, these disagreements provide a suggestive indication of how, by widening the range of tours and holiday homes available, the Polytechnic risked alienating at least part of its own community. The continuing promotion of the tours as 'educational' provided a useful stick, with which some Polytechnic members could beat its leaders for not giving more time and resources to other projects.

As we saw previously, the early Polytechnic tours to Switzerland and Paris in 1888 and 1889 had educational origins. As the touring operations grew, the Polytechnic continued to use educational purposes to justify their holidays. The earliest surviving brochure, from 1895, gives a flavour of the promotional tone, and of how it sought to reinforce the Polytechnic's hard-earned reputation. As mentioned in an earlier chapter, the committee claimed to be 'the pioneers of the now popular "Co-operative and Educational Holiday Movement" And… the first to offer facilities for Continental Travel at such reduced rates as to enable many of limited means to take a holiday abroad.'

The claim to be 'pioneers' in this area fitted well with the identity and origins of the Polytechnic, the first such institution in the country which had inspired the creation of other Polytechnics since the early 1890s. The curriculum included some distinctively 'feminine' subjects and in some cases allowed women to study alongside men. In February 1896, the Great Hall hosted a demonstration of a 'Cinematographe' by Louis Lumière, the first-ever show of moving pictures to the public. Appropriately for an institution promoting travel, the images included trains arriving and departing from railway stations. (The cinema has recently been revived by the University of Westminster as 'the birthplace of British cinema'.) In sport, Lord Kinnaird, one of the Polytechnic's leading lights and a friend of Hogg, was President of the Football Association. At the 1908 London Olympics, athletes from the Polytechnic won ten medals; the Polytechnic Harriers planned and organised the marathon, with Cycling Club members helping to monitor the race; and many competitors took up an offer of honorary Polytechnic membership and used its facilities. The Polytechnic Cycling Club began to win a string of national and international medals at World Championships and other events. In terms of travel, some 'Poly boys' exhibited what we might call *pioneering spirit* by moving abroad to join informal 'Poly colonies' of old Poly boys, for example in the USA and Canada.

We can probably read less into the claim to be 'co-operative' – except in the sense that any surplus went back to the Polytechnic rather than generating profits as such. The tours had little to do with the wider Co-operative movement, as embodied in the English Wholesale Co-operative Society, which sought to turn competitive capitalism into something more 'co-operative', based on mutual association. Peter Gurney has argued that Co-operatives wanted to 'moralise' economic relations; part of this effort involved building international links which, so it was thought, would reduce the risk of future wars. But, as the accounts of their travels show, Polytechnic tourists did not necessarily go on holiday to interact with 'abroad', or to deepen their associations with it. None the less, the use of the 'co-operative' term continued. In fairness, the Polytechnic did have links and a certain amount of co-operation with the Co-operative Holidays Association, the National Co-operative Festival Society and one or two other 'co-operative' organisations.

The trumpeting of Polytechnic tours as affordable travel was just as significant. That 1895 brochure introduction went on to comment that the tours were not for those

> [W]ho can well afford to avail themselves of the more expensive arrangements of well-known tourist agents. These tours form part of the educational work of the Polytechnic, and whilst every possible advantage is given, the committee only guarantee to give the best value for money… The tours to Venice, Milan, Italian Lakes, Lucerne, and Paris are arranged in such a manner as to offer the greatest educational inducements to participate in the same, whilst every effort is made to derive the maximum of pleasure from the various Excursions.

So affordable travel would bring the delights of the Continent to more people than ever before, while educating them and supporting the Polytechnic's wider educational work at the same time. However, while wealth was not a prerequisite for Polytechnic, respectable behaviour was. Unaccompanied young ladies 'need have no fear' as:

> In the Swiss trips a lady connected with the Polytechnic is always at the Polytechnic Chalet, and one of the Polytechnic staff will accompany each party as far as Lucerne, relieving members of that confusion and anxiety which is

otherwise unavoidable in foreign travel. The Norwegian cruises are personally supervised by one of the heads of the Polytechnic staff, who has had considerable experience in these cruises and land excursions. The Ardennes and Dutch tours will be in charge of a conductor capable of making the tour yield the greatest intellectual and physical benefit possible. The requirements and pleasures of all will receive every attention.

The Polytechnic's chartering of ships for its exclusive use would ensure that 'as all passengers pay the same fee and receive equal attention, the Barrier of Class is broken down'. In this environment, the organisers would limit or remove any threat to 'respectable' life. For example: 'Two of the greatest drawbacks to the enjoyment of a yachting cruise [have been] removed – the drinking saloon and gambling. These restrictions, although entailing a financial loss of £500 to £700 per annum, nevertheless [have] ensured harmony and sociability on board.'

The 1895 brochure included a series of appreciative comments from travellers on holidays of previous years. One writer mentioned 'chumminess … 'no extras' … a Temperance flag which banished the Furies'. Another praised their trip as providing 'a store of health for the body, instruction for the mind, and refreshment for the spirit'. In the view of a third correspondent, the holidays were 'a marvel of cheapness and management. I trust we are all better for the cruise, both in mind and body, and that we are truly grateful to the Heavenly Father for His goodness to us all throughout our voyage.' According to a fourth and fifth, Polytechnic tours were suitable for 'anyone who wishes to take a cheap, interesting, instructive, and healthy holiday'; the 'enjoyment, the health, and the educating influence of the trip were so great that a longing desire was created for its repetition …' No doubt the variety of advantages and benefits helps to explain why the tours attracted so many customers. It is noticeable how these comments from Polytechnic tourists place education as only one of many benefits, and not necessarily the main reason for their journeys.

In the section dealing with the chaléts at Lucerne, the brochure emphasised another middle-class virtue: the privacy available in the bathing house, the boathouse and in the private grounds and the promenade by the lake front. The UK holiday homes – almost all at or near the seaside – offered a seductive package of privacy, a healthy environment and sporting facilities 'reserved solely for the use of our visitors', as an 1893 *Polytechnic Magazine* article about Mount Edgcumbe at Ramsgate put it.

Different UK holiday homes were sometimes promoted for specific sections of the Polytechnic community. The aforementioned Ramsgate home was open to young men 'and a few married couples', whereas a Brighton home was advertised 'for young men' and a Llandudno YMCA property was suitable for ladies, with Mrs Edwards' Eastbourne establishment offered board and residence to ladies and gentlemen. Segregation by gender or marital status, and the significance assigned to exclusive sporting facilities and designated rooms for activities such as reading, smoking or playing billiards, bore the hallmarks of middle-class preoccupations.

There was the occasional hint that the Polytechnic wished itself and its holidaymakers to separate themselves from the 'masses', designating themselves as travellers rather than tourists, or even as 'anti-tourists'. The 26th June 1890 issue of the *Polytechnic Magazine*, which focused almost exclusively on holiday opportunities, acknowledged that 'our numbers at the Poly, are so large that there will, unfortunately, be some unable to spare even so short a time as a week on end for holiday-making'. Such members could take a train to the suburbs for any number of walking tours, avoiding the dreaded 'cockneys':

> *Within eight to fifteen miles of London there are hundreds of nooks of "real country," the existence of which is absolutely unknown to the average cockney, who, if he does go to some much-frequented rustic resort, strolls about for a few hours in an aimless, tiring way, without benefit to temper or pleasure to mind or body.*

'Recreation' in the sense of refreshing the individual was also cited as a reason for foreign travel. The aforementioned 1891 reunion report, which referred to 'put[ting oneself] in the slot' for refreshment, is a good example.

Norway was, in Polytechnic promotional prose, a symbol of escape from modern pressures. No doubt the following extract has a touch of self-satirising irony, but the sentiment is still clear:

> *The chief charm of a tour in Norway lies in … its almost absolute freedom from "the horrors of civilization" … no picture-galleries to make one's neck ache;*

no museums to make the weary feet throb; no promenades; no bands playing in the gardens; no continuation of London or Brighton … no crowds … no loafers … no mammoth hotels where you have to climb a dozen flights of stairs before you can reach your bed … no stuffy railways to whizz you past the best scenery. No wonder that Norway is becoming increasingly popular as a holiday resort for those whose ideal of a holiday – and are not the numbers of such increasing rapidly? – is to get as "far from the madding crowd" as possible.

An article from an 1898 edition of the *Magazine* suggested spending Christmas abroad was a modern response to the pressures – and advantages – of life: 'the modern method with many of us is to rush away as far as possible for a complete change after the Christmas trade pressure … taking a few days extra holiday gives the opportunity of a trip abroad.'

As the touring operation grew, facilities for the tourists advanced. By 1905, the *SS Ceylon*, the ship responsible for taking Poly tours to Norway, boasted electric lighting throughout, as well as a photography dark room and a ship's band. 'Intoxicating liquor' was still not an option, with the Polytechnic proudly stating that the *Ceylon* was unique among touring steamships in this respect.

At the same time, extended mention of the educational value of the tours became less frequent. The Polytechnic's 1908 brochure stated:

[The] *Touring Department, though carried on independently of all financial liabilities to the Polytechnic, has each year been able to hand over a substantial sum to that work* [which] *enables the Governors to keep this and the other invaluable sections of the "Poly" work in their present state of efficiency.*

This was a rather misleading picture in some ways; the tours and the Polytechnic were certainly financially connected. Equally interesting is the way in which this statement implies that the main purpose of the tours might not be educational, but to provide financial support for the Polytechnic's educational work.

Chapter 9

Conclusion: Independence and War

The First World War was not the end of the PTA story – far from it. The company continued to operate for over fifty years, making it one of the most durable travel firms in the UK, before being acquired and eventually becoming part of a famous brand (see AFTERWORD). However, the PTA's newly independent status in 1911, and the outbreak of war three years later, form a natural place for the main narrative of this book to conclude.

By the time that war came in 1914, the PTA had changed its legal status. On 29th September 1911, it was registered as a company limited by shares, the shareholders and directors being JEK Studd, Douglas Hogg and Robert Mitchell, each holding one share. Later in the year, £7,500 of share capital was raised, with 7,500 shares worth £1 each being allotted in equal thirds between the same three individuals. The registered office was 309 Regent Street (in other words, the company was still based on Polytechnic premises). The Articles of Association referred to continuing support for the Polytechnic, declaring that its objects would include:

> *To support and subscribe to any charitable and public object and any institution, society or club which may be for the benefit of the Company or its employees or may be connected with any town or place where the Company carries on business, and in particular to assist the Polytechnic Institute of 309, Regent Street in the County of London, or the Members thereof or any branch or society in connection therewith by giving donations, subscriptions or otherwise assisting as the Company may think fit …*

There is no specific document, chain of correspondence or file that states definitively why the Polytechnic chose to give the PTA private status while retaining control in this way. Part of the answer may lie in the increasing pressures relating to external funding and regulation, particularly after Quintin

Hogg's death in 1903. London County Council (LCC) began to investigate educational provision across the capital, in the hope of creating a more organised and integrated – and less wasteful – model. In 1909 its education officer, R Blair, voiced concerns that some polytechnics had made changes to their provision without consulting the council and had subsequently asked for grants in excess of what 'is contemplated by the Council's regulations'. He proposed that the Council should insist on being consulted in such cases and that polytechnic governing bodies should submit estimates for each financial year. His report recommended that the Polytechnic's university-level arts courses should cease to run as they duplicated provision at Birkbeck. Blair described the Polytechnic, slightly ominously, as a 'complex problem'. In the same year, the LCC stated it would no longer fund the social and recreational side of polytechnics, leaving funding of those activities to the City Parochial Foundation (CPF) and obliging the Polytechnic to prepare two annual sets of accounts in future.

Perhaps Studd, Mitchell and Douglas Hogg felt that remote control of a nominally private and independent PTA would enable the Polytechnic to continue to benefit from its profitability without attracting further scrutiny – and possibly punitive regulation – from external funding bodies. Whether coincidentally or not, there was less coverage of PTA activities in the *Polytechnic Magazine* after Quintin Hogg's death in 1903. The reunion event reports continued, but promotional editorial and notes on Polytechnic/PTA holidays diminished in regularity and length. An October 1910 'Gossip note' had been almost perfunctory: 'The various tours organised by the Poly for the members and public generally have been most successful, and in spite of the abnormal weather, have been more largely patronised than ever.'

In any case, the PTA continued to operate. Jimmy Sharp waxed lyrical in early 1911 about Cahirnane, the new Poly residence at Killarney in Ireland. Among other advantages of the location, 'We hope in the near future to have golf links made, and for the purpose of getting the best advice upon the same, we are trying to persuade an expert (who is prominent at the Poly) to pay us a visit.' The May issue of the *Polytechnic Magazine* related that, sensationally, Isabella Mitchell had

[B]*een tempted away from the* [Lucerne] *Chalets to pay a visit to her home. The overpowering attraction lay in her second grand-daughter. In spite of a very rough crossing we are glad to know that Mrs. Mitchell is well, and we hope that though the visit is a very brief one it has been full of pleasure. Mrs Mitchell returns to Lucerne on Saturday.*

Clearly, after over fifteen years managing the chaléts, Mrs Mitchell still felt her presence could not be spared for long. Nor was her husband diverting his efforts away from the tours. A July 1912 report confirmed he had recently returned from leading a cruise to the North Cape, many of whose passengers hailed from the USA or 'from the British dominions beyond the seas' – a sign that the PTA was building an international clientele.

Perhaps appropriately, twenty-five years after the ground-breaking journey by boys from the day school to Switzerland, which was at the heart of the PTA's origins, the 1913 and 1914 issues of the in-house magazine both reported at length on repeat visits to Switzerland by Boy Scouts. Like other Poly parties before them, the Scouts' journey was at least as much about creating their own spectacle as about the experience of travel:

They formed quite an important array, as, headed by their pipers and drummers, they swung out into Regent Street, accompanied by parents and friends, and made their way, via Bond Street, past Buckingham Palace (where to their great delight they were saluted by the Guard) to Victoria Station, where they entrained for Newhaven. The boat was full, but the sea was kind, and they made a fairly comfortable, though perhaps rather cold passage, and arrived in due course at Dieppe, where they nearly all for the first time made the acquaintance of a French train. After a more or less successful effort to sleep they arrived at Paris in the early hours of the morning, where they were met by the whole staff of the Polytechnic Officials, who had kindly and unexpectedly provided a huge char-a-banc, with some half-dozen horses and a coachman arrayed in a most gorgeous livery. In this equipage they were taken to the Gare de l'Est, where they washed and breakfasted.

In Basle, the scouts responded to their hosts' enthusiastic 'jodelling' with a Highland Fling and sword dance. Many adventures followed, with readers able to enjoy a photograph of the party crossing a glacier as so many other Poly parties had done over the years. As they crossed the lake at Lucerne in Mitchell's private launch, the band from the local casino struck up 'God Save the King' in their honour.

As the fateful year of 1914 arrived, the PTA's Holiday Tours brochure offered trips to Scotland, Ireland, Penzance and Jersey; Norway, the Rhine, Holland, Brussels, Venice, Rome, Lucerne, Chamonix, Grindelwald, Zermatt, Engadine and Paris; and (not on the cover but inside) the Isle of Man. The editorial maintained that 'These tours are organised on a Co-operative basis by the Polytechnic Touring Association Ltd and benefit the great Social and Educational Work of the Polytechnic'. A section on the history of the PTA – a sign of confidence – also alluded to its educational origins.

The brochure boasted that over 16,000 people went on the continental tours each year, with 8,500 choosing Switzerland, 2,000 going to Scotland, 2,000 visiting Paris, 1,000 opting for the Rhine and 'large numbers' travelling with the PTA to Norway, Cornwall, Ireland, Holland, the Tyrol, Italy and Spain. Perhaps as a reminder of the PTA's independent legal status, the firm still felt the need to point out that the tours were 'carried on independently of all financial liabilities to the Polytechnic', with the Board of Education, London County Council and City Parochial Foundation 'largely' providing for the 'vast educational work, whilst the results of the Holiday Tours and private donations enable the Governors to keep this and the other invaluable sections of the "Poly" work in their present state of efficiency.' As other signs of continuity, the brochure included over ten pages of information and tour options for Lucerne, where travellers could stay for a week for five guineas and two weeks for seven guineas – prices more or less identical to their late nineteenth century equivalents.

Two other items from 1914 survive: a passenger list for a cruise to the western fjords of Norway between 27th June and 10th July and a dinner menu. The cruise manager was named as a Samuel Beckett (perhaps a worry for passengers who preferred their cruises without drama) while the cruise director was William Lazarus (a more encouraging hint that the PTA would return after the war). The tour conductor was JH Deas, who had by now been hosting Poly or PTA holidays for over two decades. The menu, for dinner on 5th July, reveals that passengers could start with *consommé a la d'artois* and follow it with boiled cod in parsley sauce, lamb cutlets with green peas and mashed potatoes, braised York ham and spinach or beef *a la mode* with baked and new potatoes and cauliflowers. Plum pudding in a sweet sauce, Italian pastry, biscuits and cheese rounded off the meal. Clearly PTA passengers would not want for good food on their journey.

A vignette of PTA touring on the eve of war is available, courtesy of the letters of Walter William Ivory (1874–1944). Ivory joined up in early 1915 and became a sapper in 1916, served in France and Belgium, was gassed at Vimy and was overseas with the army when his father died in early 1919, at which point he was demobbed. Ivory had married his fiancée Florence Alice Long in February 1917. In August 1914, Ivory had been on holiday at the Polytechnic chaléts in Lucerne, with Florence's brother Fred. Two letters home to Florence have survived, of which the second (undated) is both a poignant declaration of love and a demonstration of British stoicism and determination to enjoy a holiday – no matter what:

My Dear Little Floss:-

We are having about the most sensational holiday it is possible to have.

To begin with we are under martial law and are not allowed to leave Switzerland until after the mobilization. Lucerne is nothing but soldiers + baggage varied by baggage + soldiers. Still we heard this morning that about the end of the week we shall be conducted out of the country probably under military escort.

On Sunday evening just after dinner we were all startled to hear the report of a rifle. It appears that someone here crept[?] through German presumably a peasant not answering the sentinel's challenge was fired at. This morning I heard some artillery firing, but I suppose that was only practice. Yesterday we went up the Stanserhorn and were fortunate enough to have a most magnificent view of the Bernese Oberland. At first it was somewhat cloudy on the highest peaks, but a slight breeze arose and the clouds rolled back like a curtain and one after the other the majestic peaks of Matterhorn + Jungfrau came into view.

Try to get a letter through if you can so that we can get some news of events. No news is allowed to percolate through here except through German sources + that is probably censored.

Fred seems somewhat anxious to get home to see if things are alright.

We have just had a game of billiards + enjoyed it immensely.

I forgot to tell you that we left a party on the Stanserhorn[?] all night to see the sunset + the sunrise. I guess, however, that they must have been disappointed as last night there was a violent thunderstorm and this morning it was very cloudy and raining heavily.

I often find myself wondering what you are doing and should just like to see you.

No doubt you are thinking now of packing for Cromer + are looking forward to a jolly time.

I have sweet recollections of the little girl who was the last person I kissed before leaving England and I can see her now, as I leaned out of the carriage window, waving her hand.

Remember me kindly to all your people + tell them not to worry as we shall sure to get through all right to Old England.

Lucerne is full of Americans + English all of them clamouring for some means of exit + all waiting for their ambassador's decision.

Now my dear girl. Good bye for a time.

With deep deep love
From Will

Perhaps inevitably, as war broke out, Robert Mitchell was on hand in Lucerne, having been 'elected Chairman of the Committee formed… to take charge of the arrangements for the return of British tourists in Switzerland'. The *Polytechnic Magazine* reported triumphantly in September:

It is needless to say that with his usual energy and enthusiasm Mr Mitchell accomplished the task with the utmost success. The party that accompanied him home included a lady of 93, a baby of a few weeks, and our Boy Scouts.

The PTA would return to Lucerne after 1918, in a world changed forever. However, though the lifespan of the company did not come to an effective end until its acquisition in 1962, its most innovative and successful period was about to come to an end, as Europe went to war.

* * *

In some quarters, pre-1914 travel and holidays would go on to become, like other aspects of pre-war British life, a subject for wistful remembrance. John Buchan's 'shilling shocker' novels, in which Richard Hannay performs acts of patriotic heroism while dashing from England to Scotland to Switzerland to Norway to the Faroe Islands (and back), are one example. Another, which evokes or at least suggests the PTA without mentioning the firm, appears in Dornford Yates' 1952 fictionalised memoirs *As Berry and I were saying*, with the eponymous Berry reminiscing:

> *Those* [pre-war days] *were the tolerant days. I never had a passport till 1919. Before the first war, you could walk into Victoria Station, take a ticket for Constantinople and alight there three days later without any fuss. For a five-pound note you could spend a whole week at Lucerne. The journey both ways was included and so were all sorts of excursions about the Lake. And fed like a fighting cock… Is anyone going to deny that those were the days?*

None of Berry's audience dissents from this summary. Post-1945 rationing and travel restrictions may have been contributing factors in such a rose-tinted view in hindsight. But, leaving understandable nostalgia aside, how are we to assess the significance of the Polytechnic and its creation, the PTA, in the years before war broke out?

There is no doubt that the Polytechnic was at the right place at the right time. London's growing attractions as a magnet for jobseekers, including emerging new categories such as clerks, along with its transport connections to the rest of the country and to continental Europe gave the Polytechnic immediate advantages. In Quintin Hogg it had not only a founder and benefactor but also a champion of travel; without his support it seems inconceivable that organised tours would ever have started. In Robert Mitchell it had an organiser and promoter of enormous energy; the key expeditions to Switzerland in 1888, Paris in 1889 and Chicago in 1893, as well as the purchase of chaléts in Lucerne, were Mitchell's triumphs. Toynbee Hall, although based in London, did not have an equivalent of Mitchell, which may explain why its tours were on a smaller scale. Nonetheless, the Polytechnic and its emerging travel operations were not unique. Toynbee, the CHA and other firms may have been different in the details of their origins, but we can see them all as sharing a broadly 'rational recreation' agenda, at least at first. The Polytechnic had a team of teaching staff to help lead the tours; it had a large captive market in terms of its members and students before it began to sell tours to others. If the tours had lost money, maybe Hogg would have covered the losses as he covered losses in other parts of the Polytechnic's operations. So, the conditions for the birth and growth of the PTA were favourable in many ways. The Polytechnic priced its tours – or most of them – keenly to ensure they remained accessible to the original middle class and lower middle class market.

The travel accounts of Polytechnic tourists give us an insight into a distinctively 'Poly' way of looking at the outside world. Tourists were not merely observers, but the heroes of their own narratives, bonding together on the outward journey with games and singing and noting the reactions of the local populace to their arrival. Reports of interactions with the prominent citizens of Bergen, the Prince of Naples and (indirectly) the German Emperor demonstrated a taste for mixing with higher social classes than those from which most Polytechnic tourists originated.

Polytechnic writers emphasised the significance of the tours, both on their own terms and by the citing of specific incidents and achievements, as reinforcing the collective ego of the institution itself with its record-breaking, pioneering qualities. Summaries of the joys of walking through the natural wonders of Switzerland and Norway had more than a touch of the sublime about them and also echoed late eighteenth century anti-conquest travel writing in mostly leaving natives out of the picture. When they gave attention to the characteristics of the local populaces of the places they visited, Polytechnic tour accounts placed foreigners in a pre-modern (and, in the case of the French, a rather negative) light. On tours of Scotland and Ireland, Polytechnic writers showed little interest in the locals save, perhaps, for confirming their existing preconceptions about the poverty of the Irish. A typical Polytechnic travel author retained a distinctly superior attitude to other races, although he was willing in some cases such as the Swiss and the Norwegians to offer qualified praise. This contrasted significantly both with Toynbee and CHA writers, who lauded qualities of cleanliness, prosperity, courtesy and kindness in foreign peoples.

Perhaps the most distinctive, and the most 'modern', quality of Polytechnic tours as depicted in their travel writing was a sheer capacity for enjoyment, in a somewhat introspective sense. The tour parties showed little interest in the local peoples: they were too busy fishing, swimming, walking, climbing, playing sports, teasing local policemen and each other and getting into scrapes. While this behaviour was not disreputable or 'unrespectable', it was some way from what we might expect from 'rational' holidaymakers in an era in which holidays still had, notionally at least, serious purposes.

Perhaps the best parallel to Poly touring parties in fiction lies not in Buchan or Yates, but in *Three Men on the Bummel* (1900), Jerome K Jerome's sequel to *Three Men in a Boat*. In *Bummel* (a term which J, the narrator, defines as 'a journey, long or short, without an end'), the same three men who travelled along the Thames decide to try a cycling holiday in the Black Forest. J is a writer and George works in a bank – jobs that might make them plausible Poly members or students in real life – while Harris's occupation remains a mystery. The trio embark on their tour as an escape, particularly from J and Harris's wives. Although *Bummel* concludes with two quasi-serious chapters analysing Germany and the Germans, it is for the most part a tale of scrapes and japes. J warns the reader early on that 'nothing in the nature of practical information will be found, if I can help it, within these pages. There will be no description of towns, no historical reminiscences, no architecture, no morals.' The funniest chapter finds the three men between Nuremberg and the Black Forest, where J gets into trouble for allegedly stealing a bike and George pays heavy fines for travelling on a train without the appropriate ticket. J concludes that:

> *Reflecting on the ease and frequency with which one gets into trouble here in Germany, one is led to the conclusion that this country would come as a boon and a blessing to the average young Englishman... [to whom L]ife in London is a wearisome proceeding. The healthy Briton takes his pleasure lawlessly, or it is no pleasure to him. Nothing that he may do affords to him any genuine satisfaction. To be in trouble of some sort is his only idea of bliss. Now, England affords him small opportunity in this respect; to get himself into a scrape requires a good deal of persistence on the part of the young Englishman.*

This seems to offer a neat summary of exactly why so many Poly holidaymakers enjoyed not only getting into 'scrapes', but recounting them afterwards. To be sure, the Poly tourists' travel accounts noted the important architectural and historical sights, duly ticking them off as cultural capital accumulated, preserving the impression of tours which improved those who went on them. Nonetheless, fun and enjoyment were the key rather than conformity. The observation by

Wilfred Bryant, who travelled with a Polytechnic tour but was not part of a Polytechnic party, of the absence of overt religious devotion is suggestive. Clearly there is a limit to which historians can see into the hearts and minds of late Victorian and Edwardian men and discern the extent of their religious faith; and the materials on which this analysis is based were almost all of a mediated nature, being articles in an in-house magazine. Even so, Bryant's comments, and the relative absence of religiously related matter in Polytechnic travel accounts, suggest that churchgoing and cathedral visiting might have been the 'done thing' rather than evidence of true religious devotion.

In assessing the Polytechnic and PTA's significance between the late Victorian years and the outbreak of the Great War, we should be careful not to take the institutions or their representatives too much at their own face values. The Polytechnic and PTA did not originate 'mass travel', new destinations, new methods of travel or new pricing or marketing techniques. In this sense, they were not travel pioneers in the way that Thomas Cook had been earlier in the nineteenth century. Nonetheless, they were large, significant players in a growing marketplace. Quintin Hogg, his lieutenants and his successors deserve credit for helping to make holidays affordable and accessible for more working people than ever before. Once they got there, the Polytechnic and PTA tourists enjoyed themselves in ways which may seem surprisingly familiar to the holidaymakers of today.

Chapter 10

Afterword

Two world wars, one famous brand

The PTA effectively closed down for the duration the First World War, returning soon after peace did. As for many sectors of the economy, the period after 1918 presented dangers as well as opportunities.

The PTA had to adapt to a post-war world in which, as Charles Mowat put it, 'Things seemed the same but were not'. While these trends are hard to quantify, the secularisation of British society began to gather pace, with falling attendances at Church of England services which only just exceeded the figures for Catholic services by the 1930s and falling Sunday school attendance figures. As gambling on sport became increasingly popular, the National Anti-Gambling League condemned the habit as 'un-Christian'.

There were major economic downturns in the early 1920s and in 1929–1933, affecting various parts of Britain particularly badly (for example, the North-East of England). Nonetheless, taking the UK as a whole, the interwar era was nonetheless one of generally increasing prosperity, available leisure time and leisure-related spending. Spending on admissions to cinemas, theatres and sports events rose fifteen per cent and there were increases in the sales of daily national newspapers and radio licences. Four million manual workers received paid holiday in 1938, compared with one million in 1920. The PTA, CHA and Holiday Fellowship (an off-shoot of the CHA) had to compete not only with the eternal Thomas Cook but with the Workers' Travel Association, the Youth Hostels Association, the Camping Club of Great Britain, Pickfords and others such as the National Association of Local Government Officers (NALGO).

After the glory pre-1914 days of Quintin Hogg, Robert Mitchell and JEK Studd at the helm, the PTA now had to find a new Managing Director. As Mitchell neared retirement and JEK Studd devoted time to his duties as a Senior Sheriff in the City of London, Studd's son Ronald (1889–1956) left a career in the Navy at his father's request to run the company, becoming MD in 1924.

He bought out Mitchell's interest in the PTA in 1929, at which point Mitchell ceased to be a Director. Major Thomas Worswick was added as a Director in 1926, but died in 1932. Ronald's brother Eric (1887–1975) became a Director in February 1939. Ronald remained as MD till his death in 1956 and the bulk of shares in the PTA was owned by a combination of Studds and Hoggs until its acquisition in 1962.

In contrast with the popularity of northern European holiday destinations in the PTA's earliest days, by the 1920s there was greater interest in the southern part of the continent, partly due to the rise of sunbathing. As Robert Graves and Alan Hodge noted, sunbathing was originally found useful in Germany (irony of ironies) 'to cure children of 'deficiency diseases' caused by the British blockade and by the severities of the post-war years'. But the British quickly followed suit in seeking out the sun for their holidays. Transportation trends affected how they got to their holiday destinations, with motorcar, coach and air tours beginning to feature. Private car ownership, no longer an elite preserve, passed the one million mark by 1930. The post-war era saw the birth of commercial airways, with daily flights between Hounslow and Paris from 1919 (two or three passengers at first) and internal British Isles flights well-established by 1930. More than 160,000 passengers flew between Britain and Europe by 1938, compared with 42,000 in 1930.

Ronald Studd claimed, years later, that the PTA had been 'in a sorry state … [it] was being hawked around the City and no one would buy it.' The firm's Regent Street operations were 'antique … redundant … dusty', and the Lucerne chalets lacked electric lighting, and hot and cold running water in the bathrooms. Whatever the truth of these statements (and of course Studd had a vested interest in exaggerating the difficulties which he, as the new MD, had to overcome), the PTA had not waited for the appointment of its new MD to resume its activities in peacetime. The *Polytechnic Magazine* reported on a seven-day Easter 1920 trip to the battlefields of France and Belgium for a twenty-five-strong party and announced that the Lucerne chalets would be open for a week at Whitsun. The prices of these tours were sixteen guineas a head and eleven and a half guineas a head respectively – a notable increase on pre-war prices, no doubt reflecting the bout of high inflation which had begun during the war and led to a 144 per cent increase in retail prices since 1913. Easter destinations for 1921 included Paris and Rome as well as Lucerne and battlefield tours were repeated that year.

The company gradually began to try to adapt to the changed post-war world. Its 1923 brochure of spring and summer tours included motor tours of the Loire Valley and Switzerland, and car excursions to Fountainebleau and Versailles for tourists visiting Paris. Motor tours took up more space in the brochures as time went on, as did references to the sun and the benefits of sunshine. By 1935, 'sunny Spain' featured in the portfolio, as did Nice, whose virtues were 'Almost perpetual sunshine, warmth and colour …' Tourists to Menton in France could be confident of a sunny holiday, it seemed; the PTA offered a full day's refund if it rained for half an hour or more. This was not necessarily a PTA wheeze, as a rival travel agent, George Lunn, had come up with the idea previously. Ronald Studd was keen to continue to present the firm as one that pioneered, in continuity with its early years. In 1932 it promoted what it described as 'the first escorted tour by air to Switzerland'. Much later, when he came to write his memoirs, published in 1950 as the immodestly titled *The Holiday Story*, Ronald Studd suggested that the motivation for these early air tours was a patriotic wish to keep British money circulating within British firms, rather than paying Continental railway operators to transport holidaymakers. The firm itself admitted that 'the time [may not have been] ripe… for a general extension of this kind of holiday'.

Ronald Studd decided not only to shift the PTA's emphasis to some extent towards sunshine holidays and motor tours, but also to spend money on display advertising, to appoint a general manager, to create a plans division and to expand operations in Belgium. Switzerland, where operations also grew, remained the leading PTA location outside the UK. Substantial numbers of tour options were offered for France, Belgium and Italy and, from the mid-1930s, an increasing number of tours devoted to Germany. Norway, so prominent in the Polytechnic tours pre-1911, barely featured by the late 1930s. The 'Jubilee Programme' of 1938, running to over 200 pages, featured 'special interest tours' to eastern Europe and, for £134 2s for cabin class, £88 17s for tourist class or £71 9s 6d for third class, a three week tour of Canada and the USA.

Links with the Polytechnic continued, though they were weaker by now. The PTA remained as a tenant in Polytechnic buildings, moving to Balderton Street in 1930, and made financial 'donations' to the Polytechnic each year. The *Polytechnic Magazine* continued to carry advertising and editorials for PTA tours – though the tone and content was some way removed from the educational and moral purposes which Quintin Hogg had originally subscribed to the tours. One double page spread did mention 'TRAVEL – AS A MEANS OF EDUCATION', with travel aiding 'the peace of the world [by helping] nation [to] learn to understand nation'. However, for the most part, the editorials focused on practical matters, answering travel-related questions from unnamed correspondents and featuring different destinations each month.

The PTA's 1930s brochures for UK holidays, foreign destinations and (from the mid-1930s) air tours also emphasised the practical and material. Their keynotes were the personal service a PTA client could expect, and 'comfort and economy in travel'. Late 1930s brochures provided brief profiles of some of the resident hosts, highlighting their personal qualities and interests, whether they were lecturers, mountaineers or, in the case of Hugh Pollock at Assmannshausen in Switzerland, 'a good linguist and an expert ballroom dancer.' The 1933 Summer Tours brochure was entitled 'Beating the rate of exchange'; on the other hand, the 1937 Summer Programme referred to the rising value of the pound opening up Europe, with cheaper prices than last year as a result. Overall, the same triumvirate of factors – price, facilities and social norms – informed the PTA's holiday portfolio as during its pre-1911 Polytechnic days. There was one nod to the PTA's educational origins; in various 1930s brochures, over a dozen PTA hosts were listed as Fellows of the Royal Geographical Society, lending an air of authority to their expertise.

The PTA's depiction of foreign places and people through its brochures showed some continuity with the pre-war period, historicising Europe in particular as a repository of the past. Italy was 'the country of Dante and Michel Angelo', filled with monuments, palaces, churches and art history. Austria and Germany were the places to go to 'sense the romance of ancient days' – except for Berlin, a 'super-modern city'. Sometimes the local people were mentioned or shown in brochures, wearing national dress or observing old customs.

The PTA's profitability or otherwise is hard to determine as, following its registration as a private company in 1911, it did not submit publicly available accounts. Survival, let alone prosperity, was not assured for travel agencies – especially in the wake of the 1929 economic crash. Studd later recalled the mid-1920s as the moment when agencies began to undercut each other's prices. Many of the principal firms, including the PTA, formed the Creative Tourists Agents Conference (with Ronald Studd as Chairman) in order to fix prices. Nonetheless, the company survived until war came once again.

The PTA suspended its operations during World War II, in which Ronald Studd served in the Navy, as he had done in the 1914–18 war. After peace came in 1945, the PTA had to deal with a challenging set of circumstances. On the one hand, Britain was still recovering from war, with high unemployment, rationing well-established and, in 1947, a year-long ban on travel abroad for holidays – one of numerous measures aimed at shoring up the currency. Meanwhile, holiday camps of the type which Billy Butlin and Harry Warner, in particular, had popularised were beginning to dominate the market. A 1948 survey revealed that, due to lack of capacity, over 200,000 applications for holiday camp places that year were unsuccessful.

In time, the PTA achieved a significant level of trading activity, with over 28,000 bookings and 110,000 enquiries by April 1947. In addition to resurrecting existing tours, the company ventured into the holiday camps sector, booking space in Devon, Dorset, Somerset, Kent and Lancashire, and taking over the Little Canada Holiday Village on the Isle of Wight. However, the bulk of PTA advertising continued to focus on foreign travel, describing one holiday in Switzerland as 'travel's ultimate luxury – summer holidays by private "plane"'.

By now, the company had two branch offices in Regent Street including part of the ground floor at 309 as a ticket counter, and others in Cambridge, Newcastle, Sheffield, London and other locations. Below Director level, there were now four layers of management overseeing departments for Hotels, Air/Rail, Programme Tours and Ticketing, as well as support departments: a typing pool, filing, accounts, personnel and advertising. With commercial TV and radio not yet firmly established, advertising was concentrated in broadsheet and tabloid newspapers. Meanwhile, the PTA's relationship with its parent institution became more distant. The annual donations to the Polytechnic continued, but the PTA moved its main offices out of Polytechnic property for the first time, from 16 Balderton Street to 73–77 Oxford Street. By 1953, PTA advertising had virtually disappeared from the *Magazine*, although obituaries of ex-PTA staff appeared occasionally.

As the British economy gradually recovered, levels of British tourism abroad grew. An estimated 1.5 million holidays of four nights or more were spent abroad in 1951, 2 million in 1955, 3.5 million in 1960 and 5 million in 1965. In addition to more working people having increased paid leave, aircraft technology had improved during the war, making flying faster and cheaper, especially by the use of charter aircraft, of which there was spare capacity. Entrepreneurs such as Vladimir Raitz successfully challenged British European Airways (BEA)'s monopoly on the use of British carriers for holidays, and restrictions on who could be taken on such flights. Travel agents and airlines began to offer credit facilities, the government raised the foreign travel allowance to £100 in 1955–6 and extended currency allowances for the USA and 'dollar area' nations such as Canada.

The growth of competition in the travel and tourism industry was underlined by the formation in 1950 of the Association of British Travel Agents (ABTA). The new association's first chairman was James Maxwell of Thomas Cook; its first-vice-chairman was Ronald Studd, who argued that the existing Institute of Travel Agents (ITA) gave small companies too much influence at the expense of larger companies. Clearly the PTA saw itself, and was seen, as one of the larger players in the market.

Even in the late 1950s the PTA continued to operate with a mixture of continuity and some elements of innovation to respond to changing markets. In terms of ownership, the majority of shares (22,000) remained in the ownership of members of the Studd family, with 8,000 owned by Neil Hogg (1910–1995), a grandson of Quintin. Eric Studd (1887–1975) was Managing Director; his brother Bernard (1892–1962) was also a Director (as well as President of the Polytechnic, a sign of continuing links between the two bodies). On the other hand, a new brochure *European Highways* demonstrated the expansion of the firm's motor tours, offering journeys through southern, western and central Europe and even through Russia and Finland. Spain had already been the subject of its own motor tour leaflet earlier in the decade. The reclining seats and radio facilities on each coach reflected PTA aspirations to supply a comfortable environment; the on–coach bar represented a distant departure from the firm's temperance-based origins. PTA advertising at this time gave more emphasis to 'irrational' motivations for holidays, such as the chances they offered for happiness, making new friends and even finding romance.

By 1962, the PTA had caught the eye of one of the new travel entrepreneurs: Harold Bamberg, owner of Eagle Aviation. Bamberg wanted to work with a travel agent in order to make joint applications to run routes with low fares. After Thomas Cook turned down an approach, he acquired Sir Henry Lunn Ltd. Bamberg then became interested in the PTA (which had by now changed its name to Poly Travel). Through Sir Henry Lunn Ltd, Bamberg acquired Poly Travel on 1st October 1962. Bamberg and four other directors from Lunn joined the board of Poly Travel, which continued as a separate company under its own name until its trading activities were merged with those of Sir Henry Lunn Ltd on 1st November 1967. Despite Bamberg's takeover, Eric Studd and his son Robert Kynaston Studd (1926–1977) remained directors until 1967–8. Perhaps as an astute public relations move by the firm's new owners, a renewed deed of covenant in 1963 promised to pay the Polytechnic £1,000 a year for seven years.

The next three decades involved various changes of owners and directors, a period of financial losses into the 1970s and ten years in which it ceased to trade. Bamberg resigned in 1969 in the wake of the collapse of Eagle Aviation. Curiously, while 'Lunn Poly' was used as a brand name on brochures from 1967, it did not appear in legal documents until 1976 when one of Poly Travel's shareholders, Sunair Holidays, was renamed Lunn Poly Holidays. In 1981, Poly Travel was renamed Portland Camping, and showed mixed financial results before ceasing to trade in 1987 and being re-registered as an unlimited company and sold to Thomson Travel International SA in 2000. So ended the story, begun in Regent Street in the 1880s, of a successful travel firm which had brought the pleasure of holidays and affordable foreign travel to many thousands of people.

A Note About Money

It is hard to be definitive about the value of money in the late Victorian and Edwardian era, not least because of inflation and because of the pre-decimalisation (1971) system of twelve pennies to a shilling, twenty shillings to a pound and twenty-one shillings to a guinea. But it may be helpful to take £2 (at 1890 prices) as equating approximately to £232 (2016), while five guineas (1890) equates approximately to £609 (2016). You can do further comparisons and calculations at: http://inflation.stephenmorley.org/.

Selected Bibliography

Primary sources

Archives

Regent Street Polytechnic and Polytechnic Touring Association (PTA) records
University of Westminster Archives, London

- **Regent Street Polytechnic (UWA/RSP) – items including:**
- Polytechnic Young Men's Christian Institute Diary 1886–7 (UWA/RSP/P53)
- Rules of the Polytechnic Young Men's Christian Institute 1891 (UWA/RSP/P53)
- Accounts 1891–1920 (UWA/RSP/3/1)
- *The Polytechnic – its genesis and present status*, London: The Polytechnic, 1892 (UWA/RSP/P53)
- *Poly Portrait Gallery* (UWA/RSP/P53)
- Polytechnic Reading Circle Scrapbook (UWA/RSP/P157a)
- Polytechnic Governing Body Minutes 1887–1963 (UWA/RSP/1/BG)
- Polytechnic Finance & General Purposes Committee Minutes, 23 October 1891–25 April 1900 (UWA/RSP/1/FP)
- Candidate records:
  - *Polytechnic Young Men's Christian Institute* (UWA/RSP/P106A)
  - *Polytechnic Young Woman's Christian Institute* (UWA/RSP/P107A)
- Report from Gerard van de Linde to Hogg, 17 July 1883 (UWA/RSP/P92A)
- Letter from Quintin Hogg to the Secretary, Charity Commission, 13 November 1894 (UWA/RSP/3/4 [ST45/15/16])
- Letter to AC Kay, Charity Commissioners, 5 February 1905 (UWA/RSP/3/4)

Polytechnic Touring Association (UWA/PTA) - items including:
- Correspondence relating to a complaint from Thomas Cook, 1896–1897 (UWA/PTA/1/2)
- Accounts and balance sheets 1895–1911 (UWA/PTA/1/5)
- Copies of Companies House information (UWA/PTA/1/7)
- Brochures, leaflets, guidebooks, leaflets and postcards 1897–1958 (UWA/PTA/2)
- Reunions (UWA/PTA/3)
- Memorabilia (UWA/PTA/4)
- Photographs (UWA/PTA/5)
- Diaries of Wilfred Bryant 1905–1919 (UWA/PTA/BRY1 and UWA/PTA/BRY/2)

Home Tidings, later *Polytechnic Magazine*:
- Issues from 1879–1965 (PDFs available online at http://westuni.websds.net)

Polytechnic touring brochure
British Library
- *The Polytechnic Co-operative and Educational Holiday Tours Programme 1895*

PTA incorporation
Companies House, London

Various including:
- *Certificate of Incorporation*, 29 September 1911 (cert. No. 117855)
- Articles & Memorandum 1911–24, 1926–58, 1971–81, 1981–2000
- Annual Returns (in part or in full) 1915, 1924, 1932, 1950, 1959, 1968, 1974–2001
- Mortgages 1923–63
- Registers of Directors or Managers and notices of New Directors appointed 1926, 1929, 1932, 1951, 1957, 1960, 1962, 1963, 1966, 1967, 1968
- Extraordinary General Meeting held 27 February 1963
- Annual accounts 1968–77
- Directors' Reports 1968–72

Copies available at the University of Westminster Archives ref. UWA/PTA/1/7

Account of a PTA trip to Switzerland
National Library of Scotland, Edinburgh
- 'Our Trip to Switzerland with the Polytechnic Touring Association' typescript account of a trip, probably undertaken in 1911, by some friends of Isabella Plumb (ref. 12680, item 27)

Letters of WW Ivory
Centre for Buckinghamshire Studies, Aylesbury
- Papers of WW Ivory of Chesham including letters home from 1914 (D/X/712/1-8)

PTA ownership of Highland Hotel, Fort William, Scotland
Lochaber Archive Centre, Fort William
- *Valuation Rolls for the County of Inverness – Parish of Kilmallie* 1911–2; 1912–3; 1962–3

Correspondence relating to the Polytechnic Chalets at Lucerne
Staatsarchiv Luzern, Switzerland
- Various correspondence (ref. SAL)

Thomas Cook records
Thomas Cook, Peterborough
- Holiday brochures 1889–1939
- Travellers' guidebooks, 1874 to the present
- Travel accounts, 1869–1912
- *The Excursionist* and its successor *The Traveller's Gazette* (Thomas Cook magazines), 1889–1909
- Dean & Dawson including:
  - Holiday brochures 1901–1909, 1920–1927
  - Board minutes 1904–1905
  - *World Travel Gazette* 1902–1909, 1923–1924
- *The Polytechnic Co-operative and Educational Holiday Tours Programme 1897* – various copies with bespoke front covers

Countrywide Holidays Association (formerly Co-operative Holidays Association) records
Greater Manchester County Record Office
- General committee minute books 1895–1987 (B/CHA/ADM/1)
- *Comradeship*/CHA Magazine 1907–1980 (B/CHA/PUB/1)
- General circulars/annual brochures 1900–1994 (B/CHA/PUB/4)

Holiday Fellowship records
Holiday Fellowship archive, Newfield Hall, Malhamdale
- Brochures 1926–1963
- *Over the Hills* 1920–1940
- CHA photograph album 1911–1912

Toynbee Travellers' Club records
Toynbee Hall, London
- *The Toynbee Record* 1892–1914
- Travel accounts produced in self-contained albums and booklets, 1887–1911, including a journal of the 1901 trip to Sicily
- Uncatalogued documents of Thomas Barratt including *Expedition Germany* (1903)

Toynbee Hall, Toynbee Travellers' Club and other items
London Metropolitan Archives
- **Toynbee Hall and Toynbee Travellers' Club:**
  - *Logbook of expedition to Florence, March and April 1888* (A/TOY)
  - *Log of the Expedition to Siena, Perugia, Assisi, Easter 1890* (A/TOY/12/2)
  - *Toynbee Travellers' Club 1888–1913* (A/TOY)
  - J Mallon, *Toynbee Hall past and present* (date of publication unknown, A/TOY/21/4)
  - *Residence in Toynbee Hall* (A/TOY/21/23)
  - *Toynbee Hall general information* (1906, A/TOY/21/1)
  - *Jubilee Report* (1934, A/TOY/21/8)

Memoirs and articles from key players:
Leonard, T Arthur, *Adventures in holiday making: Being the story of the Rise and Development of a People's Holiday Movement* (London: Holiday Fellowship, 1934).
Lunn, Sir Henry, 'The Polytechnic Invasion of Norway', in *Review of Reviews* vol. 4 (London, 4 August 1891), 181–4.
Stead, WT, 'Co-Operative Travelling: The Work of the Toynbee Travellers' Club and the Polytechnic Cheap Trips', in *Review of Reviews* vol. 5 (London, June 1892), 619–32.
Studd, Ronald, *The Holiday Story* (London: Percival Marshall, 1950).

Newspapers:
Aberdeen Journal
Belfast Newsletter
Berwickshire News and General Advertiser
Bristol Mercury
Coventry Evening Telegraph
Edinburgh Evening News
Glasgow Herald
Hastings and St Leonards Observer
Huddersfield Chronicle

Hull Daily Mail
Illustrated London News
Isle of Man Examiner
Isle of Man Times
Isle of White County Press
Manchester Courier and Lancashire General Advertiser
Manchester Evening News
Manx Sun
Monas Herald
Nottingham Evening Post
Portsmouth Evening News
Reading Mercury
Sheffield Daily Telegraph
Sheffield Independent
Sheffield & Rotherham Independent
Western Daily Press
Western Morning News
Western News

Secondary sources

Bailey, Peter, *Leisure and Class in Victorian Britain: Rational Recreation and the contest for control* (London: Routledge, 1978).

Barton, Susan, *Healthy living in the Alps: The origins of winter tourism in Switzerland, 1860–1914* (Manchester: Manchester University Press, 2008).

Black, Jeremy, *The British and the Grand Tour* (Beckenham: Croom Helm, 1985).

Bowley, AL, *Wages and income in the United Kingdom since 1860* (Cambridge: Cambridge University Press, 1937).

Brendon, Piers, *Thomas Cook: 150 years of popular travel* (London: Martin Secker & Warburg, 1991).

Briggs, Asa and Macartney, Anne, *Toynbee Hall: The First Hundred Years* (London: Routledge & Kegan Paul, 1984).

Brown, Henry Phelps and Hopkins, Sheila V, *A perspective of wages and prices* (London: Methuen, 1981).

Butler, Richard W and Russell, Roslyn A (eds.), *Giants of tourism* (Wallingford: CABI, 2010).

Clapson, Mark, *An Education in Sport: Competition, communities and identities at the University of Westminster since 1864* (Cambridge: Granta, 2012).

Crossick, Geoffrey (ed.), *The Lower Middle Class in Britain 1870–1914* (London: Croom Helm, 1977).

Dawson, Sandra Trudgen, *Holiday camps in twentieth-century Britain: packaging pleasure* (Manchester: Manchester University Press, 2011).

Fjågesund, Peter and Symes, Ruth A, *The Northern Utopia: British Perceptions of Norway in the Nineteenth Century* (Amsterdam: Rodopi, 2003).

Hamilton, Alys L Douglas, *Kynaston Studd* (London: The Polytechnic, 1953).

Heller, Michael, *London Clerical Workers, 1880–1914: development of the labour market* (London: Pickering & Chatto, 2011).

Hoppen, K Theodore, *The Mid-Victorian Generation: England 1846–1886* (Oxford: Oxford University Press, 1998).

James, Lawrence, *The middle class: a history* (London: Little, Brown, 2006).

Lowerson, John, *Sport and the English Middle Classes 1870–1914* (Manchester: Manchester University Press, 1995).

Lowerson, John and Myerscough, John, *Time to spare in Victorian England* (Hassocks: Harvester Press, 1977).

Mangan, John (ed.), *A sport-loving society: Victorian and Edwardian middle-class England at play* (London: Routledge, 2006).

Mullen, Richard and Munson, James, *The Smell of the Continent: The British Discover Europe 1814–1914* (London: Pan Macmillan, 2010).

Penn, Elaine (ed.), *Educating Mind, Body and Spirit: The legacy of Quintin Hogg and the Polytechnic, 1864–1992* (Cambridge: Granta, 2013).

Pimlott, JAR, *The Englishman's holiday: a social history* (London: Faber & Faber, 1947).

Pimlott, JAR, *Toynbee Hall: fifty years of social progress 1884–1934* (London: JM Dent and Sons, 1935).

Ring, Jim, *How the English made the Alps* (London: Faber and Faber, 2011).

Routh, Guy, *Occupation and pay in Great Britain 1906–79* (London and Basingstoke: Macmillan, 1980).

Searle, GR, *A New England? Peace and War 1886–1918* (Oxford: Oxford University Press, 2004).

Speake, Robert, *A hundred years of Holidays 1893 to 1993: A pictorial history of CHA* (Manchester: Countrywide Holidays, available from www.historyofcha.org.uk).

Thompson, FML, *The Rise of Respectable Society: A Social History of Victorian Britain 1830–1900* (London: Fontana, 1988).

Ward, Colin and Hardy, Dennis, *Goodnight Campers! The History of the British Holiday Camp* (London: Mansell Publishing, 1986).

Weeden, Brenda, *The Education of the Eye: a History of the Royal Polytechnic Institution 1838–1881* (London: Granta, 2008).

Wood, Ethel, *A history of the Polytechnic* (London: Macdonald & Co, 1965).

Wood, Ethel, *Quintin Hogg: a biography* (London: Archibald Constable & Co, 1904).

Wood, Ethel, *Robert Mitchell: A Life of Service* (London: Frederick Muller Ltd., 1934).

Wood, Ethel, *The Polytechnic and its founder Quintin Hogg* (London: Nisbet, 1932).

Index

Class, 9
    employment patterns, 9–11
    middle class, 9–10
        Brighton, 18
        Grand Tour, 1
        profile, 5
        travel abroad, 33–4
    occupational profile, 45–8
    working class, 11
        affordability of holidays, 100–104
        Clacton, 40, 77, 101–104
        holiday camps, 3
        importance of holiday, 18
        Margate, 2, 18, 100
        respectability, 12, 108
Coast, 2
    Brighton, 18
    Clacton, 40, 77, 101–104
    Margate, 100
Countries
    Belgium, 34, 122
    England, 2, 5, 18, 39–41, 77, 100, 109
    France, 2, 5, 28–32, 34, 58–9, 83–6, 122–3
    Germany, 61–2, 65, 123
    Italy, 1, 15–17, 48, 105, 114, 124
    Ireland, 41–2, 75, 90–2
    Madeira, 5, 34
    Norway, 32–4, 70–2, 87–9
    Scotland, 5, 41–3, 76–7, 114
    Switzerland, 2, 26–7, 32–4, 63–9, 113–14
    United States, 37–9, 100, 117
Co-operative Holidays Association (CHA),
    4
    formation, 16–17
    links with Polytechnic, 107
    travel accounts, 92–3

Education,
    elements to holidays, 26–7, 35, 50, 73
    holiday emphasis change, 2

    public lecture on Italian city tours, 48
    trip to Scottish coal mine, 76

Gender, 40
    female travel writers, 54, 75
    holiday home for young men, 40, 109
    Polytechnic groups by gender, 109
    tours by Boy Scouts, 113–14

Hogg, Douglas, 111
    1893 Chicago trip, 38
    PTA part-owner, 111
Hogg, Quintin, 4
    defends Polytechnic tours, 52, 105
    early life, 19–20
    home for boys, 39
    travel letters, 81–3

Lunn, Sir Henry, 16
    Norway voyage, 50
    Grindelwald conference, 35

Mitchell, Robert, 4
    1893 Chicago trip, 37–9
    early life, 20–1
    Lucerne chalets, 33
    PTA part-owner, 111
    Switzerland trip, 27

Perceptions,
    diaries of Lucerne, 66–9
    France and the French, 30–1, 83–6
    Germany and the Germans, 61–2, 65
    Ireland and the Irish, 90–2
    segregation of Polytechnic groups, 109
    travel accounts, 53
Polytechnic,
    brochures, 35–7, 114, 124, 126
    funds, 43, 111–12, 123
    government complaint, 52

holiday homes, 39–41, 77, 100, 109,
    magazine, 25
    origins, 20, 22–4
    tourists, 43, 45–8,
    tours, 5, 26–7, 35, 37–9, 41–3, 49–50, 52,
        54–5, 74, 76–8, 97–9, 100, 114, 117, 123
    travel accounts, 53
    visits, 28–32, 37–9
        holiday by proxy fund, 41
PTA, 3, 111
    See also Co-operative Holidays Association,
        4, 107

Religion, 11
    beliefs and observance, 11–12
    church attendance in Ireland, 91
    philanthropy, 11
    Sunday service on tours, 57
    thanksgiving service, 70
    tours at Easter and Christmas, 35

Sport, 10–11
    London developments, 19
    Polytechnic tours, 74, 77–8
Stead, W.T., 3,
    Polytechnic and Toynbee critique, 49–50
Studd, John Edward Kynaston (J.E.K.), 4
    early life, 21–2
    PTA part-owner, 111

Studd, Ronald, 8
    MD of PTA, 121–3

Thomas Cook, 3
    founder, 3
    Italy tours, 15
    Polytechnic complaints, 52
Tours,
    Killarney, 41–2
    Toynbee Hall, 17
    1893 World Expo, 37–9, 100, 117
    World War I battlefields, 122
Toynbee,
    creation, 17–18
    Hall tour, 17
    travel accounts, 92–3
    Travellers' Club, 4

Well being, 12
    health benefits of tourism, 2
    holiday emphasis change, 2
    rational recreation, 12–14
World War I, 122–3
    battlefields, 122
    effects on tourism, 123